Before Genesis 1:1

THE ESTABLISHMENT OF THE GODHEAD

David Abankwah

BEFORE GENESIS 1:1

THE ESTABLISHMENT OF THE GODHEAD

ISBN: 978-9988-3-0927-5

Find out more about David Abankwah at:

Website: davidabankwah.home.blog

Facebook: David Abankwah

Twitter: DavidAbankwah

Instagram: dave_christian_author

Contents

Chapter 1

WHAT GODHEAD MEANS

For in Him dwells all the fullness of the Godhead bodily;

-Colossians 2:9 | NKJV

Often we hear about the 'Godhead' or the 'Trinity.' It is one of the most important topics that many believers debate upon. Some people hold the view that it is a heresy to think that God is Trinity. Other people also think that the Trinity is a term that does not exist in the Bible.

Others also think that there are three Gods because there are three Persons in the Trinity. Others also think it is a term coined by other churches, especially the Orthodox. My questions are: What does the term Trinity or Godhead mean and is this term a dogma or a doctrine?

One thing we have to realize is that it is not a term coined by anyone to deceive us with, but Jesus Christ who came from heaven addressed this in Matthew 28:19 in plain words. He told us to baptize in God the Father, God the Son (Himself) and the Holy Spirit. If this term doesn't exist, He will never have mentioned it.

The term 'Godhead' is found three times in the King James Version of the Bible (Acts 17:29; Romans 1:20; Colossians 2:9).

In Acts 17:29 the Greek term is *'theion'*, signifying divinity or the Deity (with the definite article) – a perfect way to express the concept of the true God as opposed to the conflicting gods of Greek paganism.

Forasmuch then as we are the offspring of God, we ought not to think that the GODHEAD is like unto gold, or silver, or stone, graven by art and man's device.

-Acts 17:29 | KJV

The kindred word in Romans 1:20 is '*theiotes*,' which refers to the Creator's divine nature. God's divine essence, for example his limitless power and infinite wisdom, are showed to perceptive humanity through the marvelous works of His creation have been made clear since the dawn of time.

For since the creation of the world His invisible attributes are clearly seen, being understood by the things that are made, even His eternal power and GODHEAD, so that they are without excuse,

-Romans 1:20 | NKJV

In Colossians 2:9, the Greek theotes carries the meaning of 'Deity' or 'Divinity.' This text affirms that the fullness of the Divine nature is manifest in the person of Jesus Christ.

For in Him dwells all the fullness of the Godhead bodily;

-Colossians 2:9 | NKJV

In a more popular sense, the English term Godhead has come to represent the idea that the 'Divine' essence is shared by three distinct Personalities.

These are delineated clearly in the New Testament as Father, Son, and Holy Spirit (Matthew 28:19; 1 Corinthians 12:4-6; 2 Corinthians 13:14; Ephesians 4:4-6; 1 Peter 1:2; Revelation 1:4-5).

The term 'Trinity' which is another term for Godhead is not found in the Scriptures per se, but the idea certainly is there.

The word derives from the Latin, *trinus*, which means 'three-fold.'

In the Christian vocabulary, the idea is that of 'three' divine Persons who function as an absolute unity. This is not related to polytheism (many gods), as with the divergent, antagonistic "gods" of ancient paganism.

Rather, the concept is that of three distinct personalities, each fully share the identical divine nature (thus the sum of those distinguishing, essential, and permanent traits by which a Being may be defined as Deity).

In the Scriptures the three sacred Persons are, in a certain sense, represented as 'one' (Deuteronomy 6:4; John 10:30; Galatians 3:20; James 2:19).

They are one in nature; each shares the essence of deity. The Father is God (Ephesians 1:3); Jesus Christ - the Son, is God (John 1:1, 14; Hebrews 1:8), and the Holy Spirit likewise is Deity (Acts 5:3-4).

Any person who subscribes to the notion that neither the Son nor the Spirit is 'Deity' in nature is seriously mistaken.

On the other hand, there is another sense in which these entities are 'three,' that is, they are distinct personalities such as the soul is not the body and the body is not the spirit even though they share the same unit called man.

Since we were created in the image and likeness of God, we are also three distinct personalities.

The Father is not the Son (Mark 13:32; Ephesians 1:17), the Son is not the Spirit (John. 14:16), and the Spirit is not the Father (Galatians 4:6) in terms of entity and not nature of deity.

Those who allege that 'Father,' 'Son,' and 'Holy Spirit' are but three 'manifestations' of a solitary Divine Person in terms of entity, are deeply in error.

The term 'Godhead' is a respectable term that is not coined by any man or a church's dogma, but it is a representative concept that is taught in the Holy Scriptures as the doctrine of God.

16 Things We Need To Know About The Godhead

1. The Godhead is one person in essence, but three individuals.

Then God said, "LET US make man in Our image, according to Our likeness…..

-Genesis 1:26 | NKJV

The individuals of the Godhead that make God one, are not vague forces devoid of personality, floating aimlessly throughout the universe. They have thoughts, feelings, and goals.

God The Father

[2]Immediately I was in the Spirit; and behold, a throne set in heaven, and One sat on the throne. [3]And He who sat there was like a jasper and a sardius stone in appearance; and there was a rainbow around the throne, in appearance like an emerald.

-Revelation 4:2-3 | NKJV

God can adopt how He has to be. He can be one at a time or three at a time, or several at a time, that makes Him God. That is not our business to argue about that. Our prime responsibility is to accept who He is as our Heavenly Father, who cares about us as His dear children.

When we were lost, He didn't give up on us. He was always looking at the horizon, expecting us to return home one day. His mercy for us is so endless, and He is ready to forgive us anytime we repent from our sins. Even though He punishes us for being wayward as His children, the one He chastises is the one He loves.

God the Father is the personality of the Godhead that makes Him Authoritative. I will say He is the Head of the Godhead (1 Corinthians 11:3). He is the Person of God that makes Him a Disciplinarian.

He is the Person of God that expects us to honour and worship His Son as our only Lord and God. *The Father is kind to both sinners and the righteous.*

.....He makes His sun rise on the evil and on the good, and sends rain on the just and on the unjust.
-Matthew 5:45 | NKJV

He is the Person of the Godhead that makes God supply or serve both sinners and righteous with breath of life, rain, shine, and all physical needs.

God The Son

And I looked, and behold, in the midst of the throne and of the four living creatures, and in the midst of the elders, stood a Lamb as though it had been slain, having seven horns and seven eyes, which are the seven Spirits of God sent out into all the earth.
-Revelation 5:6 | NKJV

God the Son as the Person of the Godhead, that makes God gentle and lowly in heart. It is that part of God that makes Him so humble. Even though God the Son can bless us with material things, He is not interested in material things but eternal life.

So, if it is because of physical things that are why you are serving God, then it is not a good idea. He supplies material things for sinners too, preparing them for eternal judgement. But what He cannot give to sinners is eternal life, and that is why we serve God through Jesus Christ as the Godhead.

The Sonship Person of the Godhead, came and lived with us for 33 years. The way He was so humble, a lot of Jews didn't know that He was the same God their Fathers had been serving.

If we want to be great in the Kingdom of heaven, then we ought to take the humility yoke of God the Son and live as He did. The *Son is much interested in sinners.*

For the Son of Man has come to save that which was lost.

-Matthew 18:11 | NKJV

The Spirit Of God

And from the throne proceeded lightnings, thunderings, and voices. Seven lamps of fire were burning before the throne, which are the SEVEN SPIRITS OF GOD.

-Revelation 4:5 | NKJV

What makes God Omnipotent is His Spirit. The Spirit of God is the strength of God that can do all the impossible. It was the Spirit of God who brought the things the Word of God commanded out of nothing to pass.

He can spread Himself into seven and can come together to form as one popularly known as the Holy Spirit. He teaches, guides, leads, empowers, fellowships, and helps us testify about the Son part of the Godhead to sinners.

The Spirit of God is much interested in the just or the righteous or the unworldly, helping them to complete the journey of Christianity in holiness.

The Spirit of truth, WHOM THE WORLD CANNOT RECEIVE, because it neither sees Him nor knows Him; but you know Him, for He dwells with you and will be in you.

-John 14:17 | NKJV

2. The Godhead has infinite knowledge.

Oh, THE DEPTH OF THE RICHES both of the wisdom and KNOWLEDGE OF GOD! How unsearchable are His judgments and His ways past finding out!

-Romans 11:33 | NKJV

God the Father, Son, and the Spirit are all aware of all information. They are infinite in knowledge concerning everything in heaven, on earth, and under the earth. There is no question before creation and after creation that they cannot answer.

If we know anything, it is because we were created in the image of the Godhead in terms of what their knowledge is. Before school came into existence, there was a tree of knowledge of both good and evil in the Garden of Eden already.

What is amazing about the Godhead is that they are aware of what is going on in the life of heavenly angels, fallen angels, saints, sinners, living, and all non-living things at the same time. No information or whatsoever can escape them. Before creation, the Godhead was established in infinite knowledge.

3. The Godhead has infinite wisdom.

Oh, THE DEPTH OF THE RICHES both of the WISDOM and knowledge of God! How unsearchable are His judgments and His ways past finding out!

-Romans 11:33 | NKJV

Before creation, the Godhead was established in infinite wisdom. They all knew how to apply knowledge into action, and that is all what wisdom is about. It was creation that wisdom was displayed at its best.

God the Father knew what He would create; God the Son knew what He would do in creation, and the Spirit also knew what He would do after hovering over the face of the deep. The Godhead together knew how to play their duties in the application of the knowledge they had.

After creation till now, the Godhead has been working and without their infinity in wisdom, their roles as Innovators or Creators will not be possible. They are not counselled by any angel or man to do what they have to do. No one was there beside them before Genesis 1:1 to counsel them how to create the universe.

4. The Godhead has infinite understanding.

Great is our Lord, and mighty in power; HIS UNDERSTANDING IS INFINITE.

-Psalms 147:5 | NKJV

Understanding goes beyond knowledge and wisdom. You may know something, but you may not understand it. You may apply a certain knowledge, but you may not understand the depth of the principle behind it. *An innovation with wisdom and an innovation of understanding differs.*

This is the reason certain innovations with understanding have much quality and higher prices than others. Someone with an understanding of John 3:16 can preach and teach it for an entire year, but someone who lacks such understanding will struggle to preach and teach it for even an hour.

The understanding of the Godhead is unfathomable, and that is why His works are without tracing out or unsearchable. His ways higher than the ways of men and His thoughts higher than our thoughts depict the depth of how He applies the wisdom of His works.

"For as the heavens are higher than the earth, so are MY WAYS HIGHER THAN YOUR WAYS, and My thoughts than your thoughts.

-Isaiah 55:9 | NKJV

5. The Godhead has infinite might, power, and authority.

And what is the EXCEEDING GREATNESS OF HIS POWER toward us who believe, according to the WORKING OF HIS MIGHTY POWER

-Ephesians 1:19 | NKJV

If heaven is the dwelling place of the Godhead and then the earth is their footstool, then this greatest stature of the Godhead will also correspond to how great their strength will also be. No mortal has the physical strength or might to carry God, but all peoples are in the palm of the Godhead.

If the strongest man in the Bible (Samson) had his strength from God, then the Godhead is the strongest of all. God the Father, Son, and the Holy Spirit are the embodiment and the epitome of all strength. All the Godhead has power to command what must be done and authority over all.

Because the fullness of the Godhead was in Jesus Christ, it was during His time that evil spirits were casted from people. At first, no one could cast out devils. No wonder no witch (Exodus 22:18) was allowed to live because they didn't have the power to cast out the evil spirit.

Because God is the source of all might, power, and authority, no one can contend with Him in battle and win. He is the One who has lost no battle before. If we fellowship with Him, we will always be winner men and women in our ministries, everything that pertains to our lives, and Godliness.

Indeed before the day was, I am He; and THERE IS NO ONE WHO CAN DELIVER OUT OF MY HAND; I WORK, AND WHO WILL REVERSE IT?"

-Isaiah 43:13 | NKJV

6. The Godhead is holy.

"Speak to all the congregation of the children of Israel, and say to them: You shall be holy, for I THE LORD YOUR GOD AM HOLY.

-Leviticus 19:2 | NKJV

One of the key features of the Godhead is holiness, righteousness, and sanctification. Everything is possible with God, but what is impossible with God is that He cannot sin. But as the Godhead who has called us is holy, we also ought to be holy in all our conduct (1 Peter 1:15).

If we profess that we know God, then we need to demonstrate righteousness, holiness, and sanctification in our lives. You can't know God if you live in sin. Having faith in

God is not enough than working out your salvation in shear fear and trembling of holiness.

Staying away from sin is for our own good as Christians. Sin is deadly more than any disease we know. In fact, sin is what brought about all kinds of diseases that lead to death (Romans 6:23). Righteousness, holiness, and sanctification are the weapons or the armour of the Godhead.

7. The Godhead gives great counsel to their worshippers.

The counsel of the Lord stands forever, the plans of His heart to all generations.

-Psalms 33:11 | NKJV

Anyone who doesn't like to be advised will fall into sudden destruction. Many people have become like old kings who cannot be counselled. They think they have all the experiences they have to live their lives as they want. They think they know all things.

Many Teachers in ministry suffer from this. Because they teach others, they don't want to be taught by other teachers. Many Pastors do not know it all but instead of submitting to another Pastor who knows what they don't know, they are too proud to be taught.

Because God wants to guide us in all life, ministry, and Godliness, that is why the Bible is there as a manual for our direction. He wants us to be counselled with His word all the time. We have to read our Bibles as the written Word everyday so we can be informed and we should be counselled too with the spoken Word.

We also have to embrace the diverse modes of how we receive counselling. Sometimes we may not like the vessel of counselling. Sometimes the mode of counselling of the

Godhead through His Ministers can be by conviction, rebuke, exhortation, command, or correction, but we must embrace them all and obey as such.

8. The Godhead cannot lie.

And this is eternal life, that they may know You, THE ONLY TRUE GOD, AND JESUS CHRIST whom You have sent.

-John 17:3 | NKJV

As Satan is the Father of all lies, the Godhead is also the Father of all Truth. God the father is the Godhead of Truth (Psalms 31:5); God the Son too is the Godhead of Truth (John 14:6) and the Spirit also is the Godhead of Truth (John 14:17). As it is impossible for God to change, it is also impossible for Him to lie too.

He has told us in His Word that our words should be yes or no and not in between, because what is more than that is a sin (Matthew 5:37). What is more than the yes or no, is a lie. If we claim that we serve this God of Truth, then we have to speak the Truth and live as Truthful children.

Any double-tongued person is a liar. We shouldn't say a yes and a no at the same time without knowing what we mean. If we know nothing about what is going, we should say it as such. Truth is hard to say, and we shouldn't conceal it from anyone who has to hear it.

9. The Godhead created all physical matter. Hence, they cannot be made up with physical elements that they had created; rather they comprise spiritual or nonphysical natures.

GOD IS SPIRIT, and those who worship Him must worship in spirit and truth."

-John 4:24 | NKJV

The Godhead is not a physical matter to be created by any other Supreme Being. They are the self-existing Being who preceded before anything else. They cannot die and they cannot be destroyed. Nothing in heaven, on earth or under the earth can end their lives.

It is because the Godhead is not made up with any physical matter that is why they have eternal life within them and can give it to anyone who comes to them. God the Father has life and can give it to others. The Son has life and can give it to others. The Spirit also has life and can give it to others.

It is the Spirit who gives life; the flesh profits nothing. The words that I speak to you are spirit, and they are life.

-John 6:63 | NKJV

It is the Spirit of the Godhead that can give life to anyone they want. Anyone who serves them well can also have their Godly in the afterlife (John 3:16). Because they are Spirit, they can exist anywhere they want and be manifested to any being they want to be.

10. The existence of the Godhead is not limited by time. They had always existed and will always exist. Hence no one created them.

Blessed be the Lord God of Israel from EVERLASTING TO EVERLASTING! and all the people said, "Amen!" and praised the Lord.

-1 Chronicles 16:36 | NKJV

God created things with time, but time does not control him. He doesn't see time with the lens by which men use. 1000 years are before Him as one day and one day as 1000 years. That is not the case with men and angels.

Men measure time in milliseconds, seconds, minutes, hours, days, weeks, months, and years, but God measures time in times and seasons. Because time does not control God, that was why He told the Pharisees that He is the Lord of the Sabbath.

The Pharisees, Scribes, chief priests, and the rest, wanted to control God by making sure He accept their time of worship. You can't use just one day to serve God. Anytime the Godhead calls, you must respond.

From eternity before creation and to eternity beyond the end of the universe, He will always live without the confinements of time.

11. The Godhead is God alone, no one came before them and they have no rival(s).

"Thus says the Lord, the King of Israel, and his Redeemer, the Lord of hosts: I am the First and I am the Last; besides Me there is no God.

-Isaiah 44:6 | NKJV

There is no other God beside the Godhead. If any human or spirit claims to be a god, then that person is a self-existing being. But the truth of the matter is that Genesis 1:1 tells us that it was only the Godhead who created all angels, all humans, and all things.

No one is beside the Godhead. There is no other beside God the Father, God the Son and the Holy Spirit. They are the ones who need to be worshipped. There is nothing on earth or under the earth that needs to be worshipped, except the Godhead alone.

12. The Godhead is self-existing and nothing created them.

And God said to Moses, "I AM WHO I AM." And He said, "Thus you shall say to the children of Israel, I AM has sent me to you.' "

-Exodus 3:14 | NKJV

Nothing created the Godhead, and if there is another creator somewhere, then it means that creator somewhere else is the creator. But there is no other creator somewhere else besides the God the Father, God the Son, and God the Holy Spirit.

If there are billions of creators beside the Godhead, then they should all lead to one who is the source of them all and this only source is the God the Father, the Son, and the Holy Spirit.

13. The Godhead is the Lord of all peoples and things.

God, who made the world and everything in it, since He is LORD OF HEAVEN AND EARTH, does not dwell in temples made with hands.

-Acts 17:24 | NKJV

The Godhead is the owner of all things, and that makes them Lord. Many believers read the Bible and come across the word 'Lord' but they don't value it as much as the word 'God.' If we truly understand the word 'Lord,' then we will know that everything we own or can have, all belongs to the Godhead.

God owns our ministries; He owns our wives and husbands; He owns our money; He owns our bodies; He owns our souls; He owns our mind; He owns our hearts; He owns our bosses; He owns our friends; He owns our lands; He owns our businesses; He owns our cars; he owns our houses and everything we have.

All natural and artificial things belong to God because without Him creating us in the first place, we wouldn't have been able to innovate from natural things. Having the mindset that God is the Lord of all things will make you stay humble for the rest of your life.

14. The Godhead is life and the source of it; that was why they were able to create all things out of nothing.

> **For as the FATHER HAS LIFE IN HIMSELF, so He has granted the SON TO HAVE LIFE IN HIMSELF,**
>
> **-John 5:26 | NKJV**

> **Have you not known? Have you not heard? The EVERLASTING GOD, the Lord, the Creator of the ends of the earth, neither faints nor is weary. His understanding is unsearchable.**
>
> **-Isaiah 40:28 | NKJV**

The Godhead never dies. From their time of self-existence, they are Spirits who can never die. They don't have to depend on anyone to give them life before they live. After man was created out of the dust, without the breath of God from the everlasting Godhead, man would have laid there dead.

> **Now to the KING ETERNAL, IMMORTAL, invisible, to God who alone is wise, be honor and glory forever and ever. Amen.**
>
> **-1 Timothy 1:17 | NKJV**

From everlasting to everlasting, God still remains God. His throne is an everlasting throne and no one can dethrone Him. He is the same yesterday, today, and forever. He never becomes of age. He is the same all the time, will be the same all the time, and He will continue to do His own things forever.

But now made manifest, and by the prophetic Scriptures made known to all nations, according to the commandment of the EVERLASTING GOD, for obedience to the faith

-Romans 16:26 | NKJV

15. The Godhead is immortal who dealt in the light that no man or mortal could approach.

Who alone has immortality, dwelling in UNAPPROACHABLE LIGHT, whom no man has seen or can see, to whom be honor and everlasting power. Amen.

-1 Timothy 6:16 | NKJV

Before you can approach the Godhead unless they have decided that they want to reveal themselves to you, otherwise, you can't approach them without their permission.

Neither the four-living creatures, twenty-four elders, nor angels in heaven could approach God until He came down on earth, ascended into heaven, and He revealed Himself to them (1 Timothy 3:16).

If you are in darkness, you will be exposed by Him because He is light. If you are in darkness or you live in sin, you can't approach Him. It is only saints or sons of God like Him who can approach Him in His unapproachable light (Revelation 5:7).

16. The Godhead is the First and the Last. The first before all things and nothing will exist beyond Him.

"Listen to Me, O Jacob, and Israel, My called: I am He, I am the First, I am also the Last.

-Isaiah 48:12 | NKJV

The Godhead must come first in the lives of the people and things they have created. *They are not an option, but a necessity. They are not a liability, but an asset. They are not your right, but your responsibility. They are not what we want, but what we need.*

If we treat the Godhead as the Ones who are first in our lives, we would have made them first in the decisions of our ministries, jobs, marriages, and what we have. Because we don't revere God, that is why others don't honour us when we deserve it most.

Chapter 2

THE ESTABLISHMENT OF THE GODHEAD

²Immediately I was in the Spirit; and behold, a throne set in heaven, and ONE SAT ON THE THRONE. And from the throne proceeded lightnings, thunderings, and voices. ⁵Seven lamps of fire were burning before the throne, which are the SEVEN SPIRITS OF GOD. ⁶And I looked, and behold, in the midst of the throne and of the four living creatures, and in the midst of the elders, stood a LAMB as though it had been slain, having seven horns and seven eyes, which are the seven Spirits of God sent out into all the earth.

-Revelation 4:2, 5; 5:6 | NKJV

Before God created the universe, this was the first thing He did. He first established Himself before He established the universe. Before He established man, He first established the things man would need. If you are not first established, how are you going to establish someone else?

This is the mistake many youths do. They say they are ready for marriage, but they are not established spiritually, financially, psychologically, and emotionally. You can be matured physically by age, but you may not be matured in mind.

Before you can lead others, your leadership qualities must be developed or established first. You can't be clueless as a leader with your next move always dictated by your followers. The Creator first established Himself before His creations.

The Fatherhood Establishment Of The Godhead

A good man leaves an inheritance to his children's children…..

-Proverbs 13:22 | NKJV

A good father is the one who can pass good things from him to his children. Every good father leaves a positive legacy that stays on in the family all the time. That is one reason the Fatherhood part of the Jesus Christ (God) was established.

Before Genesis 1:1, Jesus Christ knew that the angels and humanity He was about to create would need fatherhood care and He needed to provide such responsibility for them. He knew he had to be depended on for His children's resources.

He knew His children needed Him as their head. He knew without the leadership of a Father, they would go wayward. He knew that without Him, no children can be procreated. He knew without Him, the universe cannot be founded.

He knew He had to be a Father so He would not provoke His children to wrath. He also had to be a Father so He would bring His children up in training and admonition through His Word.

He knew that He had to hold an important or distinguished position in the lives of His children and to direct them concerning His set instructions. He knew he had to be responsible for the righteous lifestyle of His children.

Above all, what Jesus Christ thought that the Fatherhood part of Him needed to be established was that His children needed to have His gene of holiness in them and that is the best inheritance they needed to have.

For the children who would have His gene or seed of holiness in them, He planned before Genesis 1:1 that He had to provide inheritance for them in New Jerusalem.

The Sonship Establishment Of The Godhead

IF I THEN, YOUR LORD AND TEACHER, HAVE WASHED YOUR FEET, you also ought to wash one another's feet.

-John 13:14 | NKJV

Before Genesis 1:1, Jesus Christ saw the end from the beginning that the perfect man He would create to be like Him in image and likeness, would sin, and He had to provide the way of restoration for them. That was why the Sonship part of the Jesus Christ had to be established before Genesis 1:1.

But before salvation could be achieved, unless Jesus Christ had to be gentle and lowly in heart. Without gentleness and humility, He would have wiped all His images and likenesses without trace, and He would have been a Fatherless God for all eternity thwarting His mission of creation.

One character that Jesus Christ had to establish as part of His Godhead was the Sonship. Without the Sonship character, God would not have manifested Himself into flesh to die and save us on the cross (1 Timothy 3:16).

The Spirit Establishment Of the Godhead

[5]Jesus answered, "Most assuredly, I say to you, unless one is born of water and the Spirit, he cannot enter the kingdom of God. [6]That which is born of the flesh is flesh, and that which is born of the Spirit is spirit.

-John 3:5-6 | NKJV

Before Genesis 1:1, God knew that after He had saved His fallen children, they needed His fellowship so they would not go wayward again and struggle with sin.

He knew His children after being saved and having no fellowship with Him would fall again. He knew His children would become orphans without His presence in them. They needed His fellowship in them so they could live their lives in holiness.

For the life of holiness to come to pass, their souls needed to be born again through the Spirit part of the Godhead He had to establish before the beginning of the world.

*The Three Persons Are Not Each Part Of God, But Are Each Fully God And Equally God

Within God's one undivided being, there is an 'unfolding' into three interpersonal relationships such that there are three Persons.

The distinctions within the Godhead are not distinctions of his essence and neither are they something added onto his essence, but they are the unfolding of God's one, undivided being into three interpersonal relationships such that there are three real Persons.

Understanding The Godhead

Illustrating the Godhead is a noble goal, but it is ultimately an exercise in futility. Theologians through the centuries have wracked their brains in a quest to plan a doctrinally sound, fully satisfying illustration of the Triune Godhead. What stymies their efforts is the fact that God is transcendent, and some of His qualities are unknowable.

Trinity is the theological term applied to God to show His perpetual existence as three distinct Persons (Father, Son, and Holy Spirit) who remain one indivisible God.

The concept of a Triune God is more than difficult to comprehend – it is impossible to comprehend, because we have nothing in our world that has a corresponding existence.

Humans, the most complex creatures we know of, exist as single persons, not as unified multiples because we are images and likenesses of God.

There are many ways or examples you can also try to understand with, but we cannot fully understand perfectly with our finite mind who the infinite God is.

[7]"Can you search out the deep things of God? Can you find out the limits of the Almighty? [8]They are higher than heaven - what can you do? Deeper than Sheol - what can you know? [9]Their measure is longer than the earth and broader than the sea. [10]"If He passes by, imprisons, and gathers to judgment, then who can hinder Him?

-Job 11:7-10 | NKJV

Though it is quite impossible to grasp the totality of the principle of the Godhead with the finite mind, however, we can understand the concept and know it is the clear teaching of the Word of God and some other human ways of definitions.

God Is Not One Person Who Took Three Consecutive Roles

That is the heresy of modalism. The Father did not become the Son and then the Holy Spirit. Instead, there have always been and always will be three distinct persons in the Godhead.

Is the Trinity Contradictory?

This leads us to investigate more closely a very helpful definition of the Trinity: God is one in essence, but three in Person. This formulation can show us why there are not three Gods, and why the Trinity is not a contradiction.

In order for something to be contradictory, it must violate the law of non-contradiction. This law states that A cannot be both A (what it is) and non-A (what it is not) at the same time and in the same relationship.

In other words, you have contradicted yourself if you affirm and deny the same statement. For example, if I say that the moon is made entirely of cheese but then also say that the moon is not made entirely of cheese, I have contradicted myself.

Other statements may at first seem contradictory but are really not. Theologian R.C. Sproul cites as an example Dickens's famous line, '*It was the best of times, it was the worst of times.*'

Obviously, this is a contradiction if Dickens means that it was the best of times in the same way that it was the worst of times. But he avoids contradiction with this statement because he means that in one sense it was the best of times, but in another sense, it was the worst of times.

Carrying this concept over to the Trinity, it is not a contradiction for God to be both three and one because he is not three and one in the same way. He is three in a different way than He is one.

Thus, we are not speaking with a forked tongue - we are not saying that God is one and then denying that He is one by saying that He is three. This is very important: God is one and three at the same time, but not in the same way.

How is God one? He is one in essence. How is God three? He is three in Person. Essence and person are not the same thing. God is one in a certain way (essence) and three in a different way (person).

Since God is one in a different way than He is three, the Trinity is not a contradiction. There would only be a contradiction if we say that God is three in the same way that He is one.

So, a closer look at the fact that God is one in essence but three in person has helped to show why the Trinity is not a contradiction. But how does it show us why there is only one God instead of three? It is very simple: All three Persons are one God because, as we saw above, they are all the same essence.

'Essence' means the same thing as 'being or deity.' Thus, since God is only one essence; He is only one being (deity), not three (different deities). This should make it clear why it is so important to understand that all three Persons are the same essence (one deity).

For if we deny this, we have denied God's unity and affirmed that there is more than one being of God (thus, there is more than one God).

What we have seen so far provides a good basic understanding of the Trinity. But it is possible to go deeper. If we can understand more precisely what is meant by essence and person, how these two terms differ, and how they relate, we will then have a more complete understanding concerning it and that calls in for the illustrations of the Godhead for additional understanding in the next chapter.

1

---

*Matt Perman. *What Is the Doctrine of the Trinity?* Retrieved from January 23, 2006 from: https://www.desiringgod.org/articles/what-is-the-doctrine-of-the-trinity

Chapter 3

ILLUSTRATIONS OF THE GODHEAD

Jesus used this ILLUSTRATION, but they did not understand the things which He spoke to them.

-John 10:6 | NKJV

[1]Trinitarian Illustrations?

There are many illustrations which have been offered to help us understand the Godhead. While there are some illustrations which are helpful, we should recognize that no illustration is perfect. Unfortunately, there are many illustrations which are not simply imperfect, but in error.

One illustration to beware of is the one which says, '*I am one person, but I am a student, son, and brother. This explains how God can be both one and three.*' The problem with this is that it reflects a heresy called **modalism**.

We are one as God is, but the body does not play the role of the soul and vice versa. That is how God also is. The Father cannot play the role of the Son, and the Son cannot play the role of the Holy Spirit.

God is not one person who plays three different roles, as this illustration suggests. He is one Being in three Persons (centers of consciousness), not merely three roles. This analogy ignores the personal distinctions within God and mitigates them to mere roles.

Scriptural Illustrations Of The Godhead

1. The Birth Of Jesus Christ

In Luke 1:35 an angel appeared to Mary and he said,

And the angel answered and said to her, "The HOLY SPIRIT will come upon you, and the power of the HIGHEST will overshadow you; therefore, also, that Holy One who is to be born will be called the SON OF GOD.

-Luke 1:35 | NKJV

All three members or persons of the Godhead are mentioned in this verse concerning Mary's miraculous conception; the Holy Spirit, the Highest (God the Father), and God the Son.

2. The Discourse Of Jesus In John 14 And 15

In these verses all three persons of the Godhead are mentioned and often interchangeably.

The Father is mentioned in John 14:2,

In My FATHER'S house are many mansions; if it were not so, I would have told you. I go to prepare a place for you.

-John 14:2 | NKJV

the Son in John 14:11

Believe Me that I AM IN the Father and the Father in ME, or else believe Me for the sake of the works themselves.

-John 14:11 | NKJV

and the Holy Spirit in John 14:15-17.

The **SPIRIT OF TRUTH, whom the world cannot receive, because it neither sees Him nor knows Him; but you know Him, for He dwells with you and will be in you.**

-John 14:17 | NKJV

3. Creation

All three persons of the Trinity or Godhead were referred to as participating in creation. In Genesis chapter one verse number one, we see God the Father creating the heaven and earth.

[1]In the beginning GOD created the heavens and the earth. [2]The earth was without form, and void; and darkness was on the face of the deep. And the SPIRIT OF GOD was hovering over the face of the waters. [3]Then GOD SAID, "Let there be light"; and there was light.

-Genesis 1:1-3 | NKJV

The Holy Spirit in Genesis 1:2 was seen 'moving over the surface of the waters' after the creation of the heavens and the earth by the Father. The Son of God is mentioned as being a part of creation, 'His Son, through whom also He made the worlds' (Hebrews 1:2).

Both the Father and the Son are involved here. Of the Son, it is said,

For by Him all things were created that are in heaven and that are on earth, visible and invisible, whether thrones or dominions or principalities or powers. All things were created through Him and for Him.

-Colossians 1:16 | NKJV

4. The Baptism Of Jesus Christ

[21]When all the people were baptized, it came to pass that Jesus also was baptized; and while He prayed, the heaven was opened. [22]And the Holy Spirit descended in bodily form like a dove upon Him, and a voice came from heaven which said,
"You are My beloved Son; in You I am well pleased."
-Luke 3:21-22 | NKJV

Here, we see the Son being baptized, the Holy Spirit descending upon Him, and the Father speaking out of heaven.

5. Paul's Benediction

In 2 Corinthians 13:14 Paul says to the Corinthians,

The GRACE OF THE LORD JESUS CHRIST, and the LOVE OF GOD, and the COMMUNION OF THE HOLY SPIRIT be with you all. Amen.
-2 Corinthians 13:14 | NKJV

He pronounces a blessing on them utilizing all three persons of the Godhead.

6. The Resurrection Of Jesus Christ

All three persons of the Godhead are seen as active participants in the resurrection. The Father raised Jesus Christ from the dead,

To you first, GOD, having raised up HIS SERVANT JESUS, sent HIM TO BLESS YOU, in turning away every one of you from your iniquities."
-Acts 3:26 | NKJV

Jesus Christ claimed He would raise Himself from the dead. He said,

[19]Jesus answered and said to them, "Destroy this temple, and in three days I will raise it up." [20]Then the Jews said, "It has taken forty-six years to build this temple, and will You raise it up in three days?" [21]But He was speaking of the temple of His body.

-John 2:19-21 | NKJV

The Holy Spirit also is said to have raised Jesus Christ from the dead,

But if the Spirit of Him who raised Jesus from the dead dwells in you, He who raised Christ from the dead will also give life to your mortal bodies through His Spirit who dwells in you.

-Romans 8:10 | NKJV

Each person of the Godhead was equally involved in the resurrection.

7. Verily, Verily, I Say Onto You

And he saith unto him, VERILY, VERILY, I SAY UNTO YOU, Hereafter ye shall see heaven open, and the angels of God ascending and descending upon the Son of man.

-John 1:51 | NKJV

God the Father is the Godhead of Truth, God the Son is the Godhead of Truth, and the Holy Spirit is also the Godhead of Truth. Anytime Jesus Christ who was hosting the fullness of the Godhead in Him said Verily (God the Father of Truth), Verily (God the Holy Spirit of Truth), I (God the Son of Truth), He was talking about the Godhead.

Non-Biblical Illustrations

[2]1. The Analogy Of Chicken Egg

One popular and simple illustration of the Trinity is the egg. A chicken egg comprises a shell, a yolk, and the albumen, yet it is altogether one egg. The three parts create a unified whole.

The shortfall of this illustration, and others like it, is that God cannot be divided into 'parts.' The Father, the Son, and the Spirit are one in essence (being and not parts), but the same cannot be said for the shell, yolk, and white of an egg.

2. The Analogy Of The Apple Skin

A similar illustration uses the apple: the fruit's skin, flesh, and seeds all comprising the apple, just as the Father, Son, and Spirit all comprise God. This illustration has the same weakness as the egg illustration, but the parts of the apple, considered independently, are not the apple. Each Person of the Trinity, taken independently, is still God.

3. The Analogy Of Shamrock

Another illustration is said to have originated with St. Patrick. As Patrick was evangelizing the people of ancient Ireland, he explained the concept of the Trinity by using a very common plant in Ireland: the shamrock, a member of the clover family with three small, green leaves on a single stem.

One legend has it that Patrick in his travels, happened upon some Irish chieftains in a meadow. It puzzled the tribal leaders about the doctrine of the Trinity, and so Patrick bent down and plucked a shamrock.

The three leaves, said Patrick, are still one plant, just as the three Persons of the Trinity are one God. Another legend is similar, except that it has Patrick teaching in the province of Connaught, where he spoke to the daughters of King Laoghaire, Ethne and Fedelm.

The shamrock analogy is perhaps better than the egg and apple analogies, although it shares the weakness of possibly dividing God into 'parts.'

4. The Analogy Of Water

Another common illustration of the Trinity involves the different states of matter (solid, liquid, and gas). The illustration typically uses water as the example: water exists as a solid (ice), a liquid, and a gas (water vapor).

No matter what physical state water is in, it is still water. Its chemical composition remains the same - it is H_2O, no matter if it's floating unseen in the atmosphere to create humidity, or floating in chunks in your tea to help relieve the humidity.

The problem with this illustration is that liquid water, when it freezes, 'switches' from liquid to solid, and, when it boils, it 'switches' to vapor. However, God does not 'switch' states or modes.

Liquid water can become solid or gas, but God the Father never becomes the Son or the Spirit. The idea that God manifests Himself differently at different times and in various contexts (like water manifests itself variously as solid, liquid, or gas) is called modalism, and it is a heresy to be avoided.

5. The Analogy Of Triquetra

Triquetra, which features three congruent, interwoven arcs, forming a triangle of sorts in the centre, is one of the analogies of the Godhead. It shows how the triune God exists as independent and as One as well.

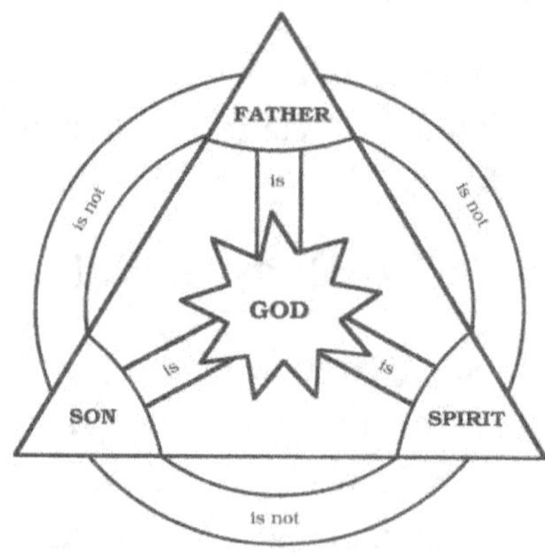

Fig. 1: Triquetra

6. The Analogy Of Addition And Multiplication

In addition, $1 + 1 + 1 = 3$. In multiplication, $1 \times 1 \times 1 = 1$. The addition shows how triune the Godhead is and how each of them exist independently as Gods. The multiplication shows how the three independent Gods exist as one God.

I don't pretend to be a mathematician, but that makes much sense to us. However, I know it is a mathematical fact. Likewise, we may not be able to completely grasp the concept of three persons in one God, but it is a Biblical fact.

7. The Analogy Of The Universe

'Uni' means one, yet the universe is made up of space, time, and matter. Take away any of the three components and it is no longer a universe. The same is true of God, take away any one of His persons and He ceases to be God.

8. The Analogy Of Government

Most countries have one government with three branches: executive, judicial, and legislative. There are three distinct parts of the one government. So, it is with God, there are three distinct persons within the one God.

9. The Analogy Of The Sun

There are three parts to the sun - heat rays, light rays and chemical rays. Heat rays are felt and not seen, light rays are seen but not felt. Chemical rays have an effect, though they are not seen nor felt. All together we have sunshine, three rays and one light.

Without one aspect, we would have no sunlight. The same is true of the Trinity or Godhead. God comprises the three distinct parts or persons, take away any aspect, and we cease to have God.

10. The Analogy Of Man

Man was made in the image of God (Genesis 1:26). Man comprises three parts. He has a body, soul, and spirit. Take away any part of him and he ceases to be man, yet there are three distinct parts to man. Man has three parts, a trinity, yet he is one man. Likewise, God is the Father, the Son and the Spirit, yet He is One.

11. The Analogy Of A Triangle

A triangle has three sides. Take away either side and it will cease to be a triangle. It's similar with the trinity (Godhead). Take away one aspect and He ceases to be God.

The egg, the apple, the shamrock, the states of matter, and various geometric shapes are as close as we can come to illustrating the Trinity, yet we cannot completely understand God's existence.

We accept the Word of God, and by faith we understand that God exists in a realm and in a manner beyond our experience. An infinite God cannot be fully delineated in a finite illustration.

2

---

[1]Matt Perman. *What Is the Doctrine of the Trinity?* Retrieved from January 23, 2006 from: https://www.desiringgod.org/articles/what-is-the-doctrine-of-the-trinity
[2]GotQuestions. *What are some popular illustrations of the Holy Trinity?* Retrieved: www.gotquestions.org/Holy-Trinity.html

Chapter 4

THE SECRET PLACE OF THE GODHEAD BEFORE GENESIS 1:1

Before the mountains were brought forth, or ever You had formed the earth and the world, EVEN FROM EVERLASTING TO EVERLASTING, YOU ARE GOD.

-Psalms 90:2 | NKJV

Many believers wonder where God was dwelling before He created the universe. Sometimes when you think about it, it challenges your intellect. Even though we should not think about things that are above us.

The thought of where God dwelt before He created the universe might have bothered the mind of a matured Christian before.

No one can tell me that before He moved into his or her own house, he or she didn't have any place to stay. Many people who own their houses today once hired someone's house, or they once lived in their parent's home before they moved into theirs.

Sometimes the time it took for them to get their homes ready, can be months or years depending on their financial muscle. Those of us who think God was probably doing nothing before He created the universe should know that the divine Creator is not a lazy God, but someone who is always working even behind the scenes.

But Jesus answered them, "MY FATHER HAS BEEN WORKING UNTIL NOW, and I have been working."

-John 5:17 | NKJV

If God ever wanted a place to stay, He didn't need anyone to help Him out. No mortal was ever there to help God build His house he had to live in, and that is why ministers have to be careful with the thought that the cathedrals they are building is a place God abides.

God, who made the world and everything in it, since He is Lord of heaven and earth, DOES NOT DWELL IN TEMPLES MADE WITH HANDS.

-Acts 17:24 | NKJV

The reason we can't see God moving physically in His state of Godhead is that He is dwelling in His secret place, and that is also why He is hid from us. Before we can know the secret things of God unless He unravels them from His secret dwelling place.

Before God created the heavens and the earth, He was already dwelling in His secret place.

8 Features Of The Dwelling Places Of The Godhead

1. The dwelling place of the Godhead before Genesis 1:1, was their secret places.

He who dwells in the SECRET PLACE OF THE MOST HIGH shall abide under the shadow of the Almighty.

-Psalms 91:1 | NKJV

There is a secret place of dwelling where God resides. Even though the heaven became His dwelling place after He created the universe, the Godhead dwelt in their secret places in eternity. Eternity, because God is not limited by time when He is dwelling in His secret place.

2. The secret dwelling place of the Godhead has a shadow saints can also dwell.

He who dwells in the secret place of the Most High shall abide under the shadow of the Almighty.

-Psalms 91:1 | NKJV

The secret place of the Godhead has a shelter called shadow of the Almighty, where saints can also dwell. If saints serve God with the chief aim of having an eternal life without the aim of loving God, we can't make it in our Christian lives.

We don't serve God with the main aim of New Jerusalem or enjoying the benefits of His promises. If we truly love God, then we will desire to dwell in His dwelling place He has created for us, which is His shadow.

3. The secret place of the Godhead has an unapproachable light no one can dwell without His permission.

Who alone has immortality, DWELLING IN UNAPPROACHABLE LIGHT, whom no man has seen or can see, to whom be honor and everlasting power. Amen.

-1 Timothy 6:16 | NKJV

The secret place where God dwelt before Genesis 1:1 has an unapproachable light no four living creatures, twenty-four elders, angels or man can approach. Even the distance between where God's secret place is, no being can approach it unless the Godhead.

Why couldn't no one approach the One who sat on the throne to break the seals of the book the Father was holding? This is because no one was worthy to go into the unapproachable light of the secret place of God.

So I wept much, because NO ONE WAS FOUND WORTHY to open and read the scroll, or to look at it.

-Revelation 5:3 | NKJV

But God the Son, who is one Person of the Godhead, went into the unapproachable light and was permitted to have the Book so He would break the seals.

⁶And I looked, and behold, in the midst of the throne and of the four living creatures, and in the midst of the elders, stood a Lamb as though it had been slain, having seven horns and seven eyes, which are the seven Spirits of God sent out into all the earth. ⁷THEN HE CAME AND TOOK THE SCROLL OUT OF THE RIGHT HAND OF HIM WHO SAT ON THE THRONE.

-Revelation 5:6-7 | NKJV

4. The duration of God's secret place He dwells in is not limited by time.

Before the mountains were brought forth, or ever You had formed the earth and the world, EVEN FROM EVERLASTING TO EVERLASTING, YOU ARE GOD.

-Psalms 90:2 | NKJV

The secret place of the Godhead has no expiry date that He has to dwell in and retire later on. He dwelt in it before eternity; now He is dwelling in it in heaven, and He will dwell in it eternally in New Jerusalem.

As men are confined by a time they have to live on this earth, the Godhead is not confined by time in their secret places. From eternity to eternity, they will always live in their secret places.

5. Before Genesis 1:1, the dwelling place of God the Father on earth was predetermined.

For I have not dwelt in a house since the time that I brought the children of Israel up from Egypt, even to this day, BUT HAVE MOVED ABOUT IN A TENT AND IN A TABERNACLE.

-2 Samuel 7:6 | NKJV

Before Genesis 1:1, God the Father of the Godhead predetermined His dwelling place on the earth with His people in buildings made with human hands. From tent, tabernacle, and finally the temple, God the Father dwelt among men in physical dwelling places.

6. Before Genesis 1:1, the dwelling place of God the Son on earth was predetermined.

But made Himself of no reputation, TAKING THE FORM OF A BONDSERVANT, and coming in the likeness of men.

-Philippians 2:7 | NKJV

Before Genesis 1:1, God the Son of the Godhead predetermined that His dwelling place would be one body which is the form of a bondservant. He didn't take any form of a Master, a rich man, or a prominent person.

This teaches us that one character of the Godhead is humility. No wonder He told us in Matthew 11:29 to take His yoke upon ourselves and learn from Him because He is gentle and lowly in heart.

Take My yoke upon you and learn from Me, for I am gentle and lowly in heart, and you will find rest for your souls.

-Matthew 11:29 | NKJV

When God the Son wanted a place to stay in men, He didn't get a place to lay His head. He had to stay in just the body he was born with because He was preparing a permanent place for the final dwelling place of the Holy Spirit.

And Jesus said to him, "Foxes have holes and birds of the air have nests, but the Son of Man has nowhere to lay His head."

-Matthew 8:20 | NKJV

7. Before Genesis 1:1, the dwelling place of God the Holy Spirit on earth was predetermined.

And I heard a loud voice from heaven saying, "BEHOLD, THE TABERNACLE OF GOD IS WITH MEN, AND HE WILL DWELL WITH THEM, and they shall be His people. God Himself will be with them and be their God.

-Revelation 21:3 | NKJV

The dwelling place of the Holy Spirit as one of the Persons of the Godhead is in the body of saints. The Holy Spirit didn't come to dwell in the bodies of sinners because they have not been sanctified by the blood of Jesus Christ.

God, the Son dwelt in one body, but the Holy Spirit is dwelling in many bodies at the same time. Anyone who is living in righteousness, holiness, and sanctification, is because his body has now turned into the temple of the Holy Spirit.

Do you not know that you are the temple of God and that the SPIRIT OF GOD DWELLS IN YOU?

-1 Corinthians 3:16 | NKJV

8. The dwelling places of the Godhead is in themselves.

Believe Me that I AM IN THE FATHER AND THE FATHER IN ME, or else believe Me for the sake of the works themselves.

-John 14:11 NKJV

We should know once and for all that, God the Father is in God the Son and God the Holy Spirit; God, the Son is also in God the Father and God the Holy Spirit, and God the Holy Spirit is also in God the Father and God the Son.

This illustrates that God is One. Spirits can spread themselves and work at the same time. The same way the spirit of Death is working somewhere to separate someone's soul from his body in location A, the same way the same spirit of Death is working at location B.

God is one in essence, but He can spread Himself into many manifestations of independent Persons to fulfil His purpose.

Chapter 5

THE ESTABLISHMENT OF THE THRONE OF THE GODHEAD BEFORE GENESIS 1:1

YOUR THRONE IS ESTABLISHED FROM OF OLD; You are from everlasting.

-Psalms 93:2 | NKJV

Before Genesis 1:1, the throne of God was established already. We all know that if someone can be enthroned by another, then he can also be dethroned by the same person or someone with higher authority.

But God was not enthroned by anyone before Genesis 1:1 that He has to be dethroned. Since the beginning to this time, we have heard nowhere that God has been dethroned from His seat. His place as our God has not changed and He will continue to be our God for all eternity.

Three Thrones For The Godhead?

"I watched till THRONES WERE PUT IN PLACE, and the Ancient of Days was seated; His garment was white as snow, and the hair of His head was like pure wool. His throne was a fiery flame, its wheels a burning fire;

-Daniel 7:14 | NKJV

Since God is one being but has three Persons that make up one being, then we may be tempted to think that each three Persons need to have His throne, making three thrones, but that is not the case.

There is one throne for the Godhead – God the Father, the Son, and the Holy Spirit. Since the three Persons come together to form one being, then there is no need to have three thrones to bring about separation, and that is why their abiding in each other makes sense.

Yet, there are two main types of thrones that the Godhead sits on and these are the *throne of judgement* and the *throne of mercy*.

From the beginning to the time that Jesus Christ died and rose again, the Godhead was sitting on the seat of judgement where grace for forgiving sins and wiping them off, began.

The Revelation Of Apostle John

Immediately I was in the Spirit; and behold, A THRONE SET IN HEAVEN, and One sat on the throne.

-Revelation 4:2 | NKJV

When Apostle John had his revelation, he didn't see three thrones of the Godhead, thus one in the middle that God the Father sits on, one on the right-hand side where Jesus Christ sits on, and on the left hand where the Holy Spirit also sits on.

He only saw only one throne in heaven where the Godhead sits on. Even though there are three persons of the Godhead, they have only one throne. This means that the God we serve is one and not three as many know it to be.

Misconception Of The Right Hand Of God

Looking unto Jesus, the author and finisher of our faith, who for the joy that was set before Him

endured the cross, despising the shame, and has sat down at the right hand of the throne of God.

-Hebrews 12:2 | NKJV

Jesus Christ, sitting at the right hand of God has become a great debate in the body of Christ that has made many people to believe that God is three and not one.

I used to believe that Jesus Christ was sitting beside God the Father in heaven on another throne. If Jesus Christ is sitting on the right hand of God in His Spirit, then where is the throne of the Holy Spirit then?

There is nowhere in the Bible that specified that the Holy Spirit has a throne in heaven. Then if two have a throne and one does not, then it means one is always sitting down on the floor or probably standing, which is not the case.

What We Need To Know About The Hands Of God

1. Jesus Christ is the Father's right-handed person of the Godhead.

In the beginning was the Word, and the WORD WAS WITH GOD, and the Word was God.

-John 1:1 | NKJV

Jesus Christ is the Word of God and He is the right-handed person of the Godhead. A right-handed man is someone who is of honour to someone. That also means that that person is also an indispensable person.

The Godhead cannot do anything without the Word of God. He worked as the right hand of God during the dispensation of God the Father. He is also working as the right hand in the dispensation of the Holy Spirit too.

2. The Godhead uses the right hand of the body of the Godhead more often, making them right-handed.

A right-handed person is someone who uses the right hand more often than the left hand. Since the right hand of God has been stressed on multiple times in the Bible, then it means the right hand of God is of much relevance to the Godhead making the Godhead right-handed.

3. The right hand of God saves.

Now I know that the Lord saves His anointed; He will answer him from His holy heaven with the SAVING STRENGTH OF HIS RIGHT HAND.

-Psalms 20:6 | NKJV

Anytime God saves, it is His right hand that does the work. His right hand has to touch the soul to bring about deliverance from sin. Anyone the right hand of God has saved cannot sin again.

4. The left hand of God gives gifts.

Since the right hand of God is the Word, then the left hand of God is the Holy Spirit. Anytime God wants to bless us with gifts, He sends us His Holy Spirit to bless us with gifts. You can have the gifts of the Holy Spirit, but you may not have the Person of the Holy Spirit in you.

Gifts can be both material (food, water, clothing, shelter, money, husbands, wives, children, jobs, lands etc) and immaterial (ministerial offices, spiritual gifts, fruits of the Spirit etc).

5. The Bible didn't say right hand side of God.

Throughout the Bible, it didn't specify the word 'SIDE,' rather, right hand of God. If the Bible added side, then it would have meant that there is another person who is at the side of God sitting on another throne.

If there was side, then we will be tempted to think that there is another throne beside the throne of the Godhead reserved for God the Son and God the Holy Spirit.

6. The right hand of God is where saints will be separated before Him in the last judgement.

All the nations will be gathered before Him, and He will separate them one from another, as a shepherd divides his sheep from the goats. AND HE WILL SET THE SHEEP ON HIS RIGHT HAND, but the goats on the left.

-Matthew 25:31 | NKJV

Since the right hand of God saves, it is where saints will be separated from sinners to, signifying that they are saved. God never destroys both the righteous and sinners together. He first has to separate the righteous ones from the evil ones before He can execute His punishment and judgement.

FAR BE IT FROM YOU TO DO SUCH A THING AS THIS, TO SLAY THE RIGHTEOUS WITH THE WICKED, so that the righteous should be as the wicked; far be it from You! Shall not the Judge of all the earth do right?"

-Genesis 18:24 | NKJV

7. The left hand of God is where sinners will be separated before Him in the last judgement.

All the nations will be gathered before Him, and He will separate them one from another, as a shepherd divides his sheep from the goats. AND HE WILL

SET the sheep on his right hand, but THE GOATS ON THE LEFT.

-Matthew 25:31 | NKJV

In the last judgement, sinners will be gathered by the four angels who hold the four winds to the left-hand side of Jesus Christ and they will be eternally condemned to the lake of fire.

9 Characteristics About The Throne Of God Before Genesis 1:1

1. Before Genesis 1:1, the throne of judgement of the Godhead was already established.

For You have maintained my right and my cause; You sat on the THRONE JUDGING in righteousness.

-Psalms 9:4 | NKJV

The throne of judgement is one of the thrones God sits. He sits there when He wants to punish someone or when He wants to judge. There is a difference between God's judgement and His punishment.

Though it seems God has judged anyone before, it is just His punishment. His judgement is so fearsome that no one can stand His judgement. His judgement even before Genesis 1:1, has been prepared for the fallen angels and sinners in the lake of fire eternally.

Glimpses of His judgement which is seen as His punishments for sinners was an instant judgement. He destroyed the whole earth by flood as His punishment and not judgement.

He also destroyed Sodom and Gomorrah by fire and brimstone, and that was also His punishment and not judgement. All these whiles, He was sitting on the throne of judgement.

When God sits on His throne of judgement, no one can plead for mercy. There is no grace for forgiveness of sins. That is the essence of why we have to give our lives to Him while we still can.

But the Lord shall endure forever; HE HAS PREPARED HIS THRONE FOR JUDGMENT.

-Psalms 9:7 | NKJV

2. Before Genesis 1:1, the throne of mercy of the Godhead was already established.

And above it were the cherubim of glory overshadowing the MERCY SEAT. Of these things we cannot now speak in detail.

-Hebrews 9:4 | NKJV

The mercy seat is the seat of grace. It is what the Godhead is sitting on right now, reconciling sinners to God through the blood that was shed by God the Son. Without the mercy seat, there cannot be mediation and hence salvation.

For there is ONE GOD AND ONE MEDIATOR BETWEEN GOD AND MEN, THE MAN CHRIST JESUS,

-1 Timothy 2:5 | NKJV

This throne was established even before the world began. God knew that man would fall into sin and he would need grace to be saved. God programmed everything, and no event can take Him by surprise.

3. Before Genesis 1:1, all languages were infused into the throne of the Godhead.

And from the throne proceeded lightnings, thunderings, and VOICES. Seven lamps of fire were burning before the throne, which are the seven Spirits of God.

-Revelation 4:5 | NKJV

The Godhead descending to make the language of the people of Babel confused and scattering them abroad with their own unique languages was not just a mere event in the Bible. God knows all languages, and it is in His throne that all languages were established before Genesis 1:1.

God gave all languages to the nations, but He reserved only one language which is the language of Christianity and that is the speaking of new tongues.

We have different tongues as a gift that God has given to the nations or can give to anyone as his or her spiritual gift, but new tongues is given by the Holy Spirit only. It is that new tongue that we will speak in New Jerusalem.

4. Before Genesis 1:1, the thrones of men on earth were already predetermined by the Godhead.

[7]The Lord makes poor and makes rich; He brings low and lifts up. [8]He raises the poor from the dust and lifts the beggar from the ash heap, to set them among princes and make them inherit the throne of glory.

-1 Samuel 2:7-8 | NKJV

Before Genesis 1:1, God was establishing the seats of men physically as the leadership of the nation such as Presidents, Ministers of State, Kings, Queens, etcetera. There cannot be any kingdom or rulership without God permitting or establishing it.

Let every soul be subject to the governing authorities. FOR THERE IS NO AUTHORITY EXCEPT FROM GOD, AND THE AUTHORITIES THAT EXIST ARE APPOINTED BY GOD.

-Romans 13:1 | NKJV

The Godhead is the head over all rulership and they determine every leadership. Even the thrones of parents who need to be authorities over us were even predetermined or set by the Godhead even before we were born.

[26]Now in the sixth month the ANGEL GABRIEL WAS SENT BY GOD to a city of Galilee named Nazareth, [27]to a virgin betrothed to a man whose name was JOSEPH, of the house of David. The virgin's name was MARY.

-Luke 1:26-27 | NKJV

5. Before Genesis 1:1, the thrones of the five-fold ministry of the church were established by the Godhead.

And He Himself gave some to be apostles, some prophets, some evangelists, and some pastors and teachers,

-Ephesians 4:11 | NKJV

The five-fold ministry is not just offices, but they are thrones. If you are not seated on any of the thrones, you will find it difficult doing the work of God. No wonder many Ministers who are not enthroned, can't bring their ministries to an expected end.

It was when Jesus Christ spoke about the throne of Moses (thus the ministry of teachers) which the Pharisees and the scribes sat on, that revealed that, ministry is not about Bible school or the work you are interested in without God choosing you, but the throne of ministry the Godhead has enthroned you on.

Saying: "The scribes and the Pharisees sit in MOSES' SEAT.

-Matthew 23:2 | NKJV

6. Before Genesis 1:1, the thrones of saints in New Jerusalem were already predetermined.

TO HIM WHO OVERCOMES I WILL GRANT TO SIT WITH ME ON MY THRONE, as I also overcame and sat down with My Father on His throne.

-Revelation 3:20 | NKJV

If we are kings and priests, then we need to have thrones because there is no king without a throne. If we will sit with Jesus Christ on His throne, then it means we will also be given thrones to sit on and be ruled together with Jesus Christ.

We are kings and God is the King over all of us. No wonder He is called King of Kings and Lord of Lords. If we successfully end our Christian journey, we will each be given thrones and crowns.

7. Before Genesis 1:1, the throne of the Godhead was founded on righteousness and justice.

RIGHTEOUSNESS AND JUSTICE ARE THE FOUNDATION OF YOUR THRONE; mercy and truth go before Your face.

-Psalms 89:14 | NKJV

Now that many leaderships have their foundation on the shedding of blood of its citizens, money embezzlements, corruption, slavery, unemployment, political instabilities, favouritism, and nepotisms, the leadership of God is founded on righteousness and justice.

8. Before Genesis 1:1, the Godhead predetermined where they will establish the dwelling places of the four living creatures around their throne.

AND ABOVE THE FIRMAMENT OVER THEIR HEADS WAS THE LIKENESS OF A THRONE, in appearance like a sapphire stone; on the likeness of the throne was a likeness with the appearance of a man high above it.

-Ezekiel 1:26 | NKJV

Before the throne there was a sea of glass, like crystal. AND IN THE MIDST OF THE THRONE, AND AROUND THE THRONE, WERE FOUR LIVING CREATURES full of eyes in front and in back.

-Revelation 4:6 | NKJV

Before Genesis 1:1, God had already predetermined where the four living creatures would sit around His throne in heaven. If you wonder what God was doing before the beginning, these were all the things He was planning before creating everything.

The four living creatures have their own dwelling places on their wheels. It looks as if their seats are found in their wheels (Ezekiel 1:15-21). They are much closer to the throne of God because they are the cabinet of God, making sure the Word of God is established.

9. Before Genesis 1:1, the Godhead predetermined where they will establish the thrones of the twenty-four elders around their throne.

Around the throne were TWENTY-FOUR THRONES, and on the thrones I saw twenty-four elders sitting, clothed in white robes; and they had crowns of gold on their heads.

-Revelation 4:4 | NKJV

Before Genesis 1:1, the Godhead already predetermined the thrones of the twenty-four elders. The thrones of the twenty-four elders are not closer to the throne of the Godhead as Revelation 4:4 narrates, but are established many distances away because of the immersive glory of God.

The work of the twenty-four elders is much centred on judgement. They sit on spiritual matters mainly concerning the church and they pass out judgement upon believers. They are the ones who spiritually excommunicate sinful believers from the church if the Pastor does not do it.

Chapter 6

THE MANIFESTATIONS OF THE GODHEAD BEFORE GENESIS 1:1

And without controversy great is the mystery of godliness: God was manifested in the flesh, justified in the Spirit, seen by angels, preached among the Gentiles, believed on in the world, received up in glory.

-1 Timothy 3:16 | NKJV

Before the heavens and the earth was created, it was God who planned its creation. That is the truth we all need to adhere to. There is no other Creator we should think otherwise. Your belief in God as the Creator or not, or no existence of God, doesn't change the Truth that He is.

The question many people sometimes ask is that, before the beginning, where was God and where was He living before He created His resting place in heaven after the beginning? That makes God mysterious.

Another mystery of God is that God is not a body and God is not a soul, but He was the Word before the beginning but His Persons has manifested themselves to us after the beginning with about seven manifestations (living and non-living manifestations).

1. The Plant Manifestation

"I am the TRUE VINE, and My Father is the vinedresser.

-John 15:1 | NKJV

God is the true vine who before the beginning, thought how He would manifest Himself to the Israelites as the rod of Aaron for the house of Levi (because He is the High Priest) that budded, brought forth buds, bloomed blossoms, and yielded almonds.

And it came to pass, that on the morrow Moses went into the tabernacle of witness; and, behold, the rod of Aaron for the house of Levi was budded, and brought forth buds, and bloomed blossoms, and yielded almonds.

-Numbers 17:8 | NKJV

God was also the tree of life that was in the centre of the Garden of Eden and the tree of life in New Jerusalem that yielded twelve fruits. He was telling us He is the central figure of the entire Bible and the entirety of our life whom we cannot do without.

.....The TREE OF LIFE was also in the midst of the garden,

-Genesis 2:9 | NKJV

In the middle of its street, and on either side of the river, was the TREE OF LIFE, which bore twelve fruits, each tree yielding its fruit every month. The leaves of the tree were for the healing of the nations.

-Revelation 22:2 | NKJV

2. The Animal Manifestation

Before Genesis 1:1, God knew how He would manifest to us in the likeness of an animal such as dove (in the form of the Holy Spirit), lion (tribe of Judah), lamb (as a sacrifice for the remission of our sins).

He was the animal that was killed, and its hide used to make clothes for Adam and Eve. You can't make tunics of skin, without killing an animal and using its hide for the dress.

Also for Adam and his wife the Lord God made tunics of SKIN, and clothed them.

-Genesis 3:21 | NKJV

He was also the ram that revealed Himself to Abraham when he was about to sacrifice Isaac on the altar.

And Abraham lifted up his eyes and looked, and behold, behind him was a RAM, caught in a thicket by his horns. And Abraham went and took the ram and offered it up as a burnt offering instead of his son.

-Genesis 22:13 | NKJV

God was the Lamb that revealed Himself to John, the Apostle. God was the dove that revealed Himself to John - the Baptist.

When He had been baptized, Jesus came up immediately from the water; and behold, the heavens were opened to Him, and He saw the Spirit of God descending like a DOVE and alighting upon Him.

-Matthew 3:16 NKJV

3. The Human Manifestation

But made Himself of no reputation, TAKING THE FORM OF A BONDSERVANT, and coming in the likeness of men.

-Philippians 2:7 | NKJV

Before Genesis 1:1, God knew that one day He would pay the sins of men with His own blood through the manifestation of the image of men – form of humanity.

The body God took to save us from our sins is what we call 'SON OF GOD.' Because man cannot see His face and live, He already planned man's redemption even before the beginning.

Before man can become like God (man in God's Spirit), he first needs to be born again through His Word. Likewise, before God could also become man (God in human flesh), He became born again through the Word.

For God so loved the world that He gave His only BEGOTTEN SON, that whoever believes in Him should not perish but have everlasting life.

-John 3:16 | NKJV

4. The Angelic Manifestation

Then the Lord appeared to him by the terebinth trees of Mamre, as he was sitting in the tent door in the heat of the day. So he lifted his eyes and looked, and behold, three men were standing by him; and when he saw them, he ran from the tent door to meet them, and bowed himself to the ground,

-Genesis 18:1 | NKJV

Now the TWO ANGELS came to Sodom in the evening, and Lot was sitting in the gate of Sodom. When Lot saw them, he rose to meet them, and he bowed himself with his face toward the ground.

-Genesis 19:1 | NKJV

God can take any form of manifestation as far as living things are concerned. In the Bible, the Godhead manifested themselves as the angel of the Lord to His people and to whom He wanted to manifest Himself.

If you are not one of those who He wants to manifest before the world began, no amount of prayers can make Him do so.

We can't command God to do something beyond His will. All those who were in His plan before Genesis 1:1, were visited by the Godhead as angels. Even if it was an angel He sent, the Word the angel was presenting was not his but the presentation of God Himself.

Many people take their dreams lightly even when they see angels in their dreams. Meanwhile, the devil can also present himself as an angel of light, but God can also manifest Himself as an angel to you, depending on the level of Christianity you are.

5. The Trinitarian Manifestation

Go therefore and make disciples of all the nations, baptizing them in the name of the FATHER and of the SON and of the HOLY SPIRIT,

-Matthew 28:19 | NKJV

The Godhead we have been talking about is Jesus Christ of Nazareth. One of His manifestations of His Persons is God the Father in the Old Testament. Another Personal manifestation of Him in the New Testament as God the Son, and now He has manifested Himself to us as the Person of the Holy Spirit.

The Trinity is the manifestation of Jesus Christ to us, but there is only one Person on the throne! Before Genesis 1:1, Jesus Christ knew the importance of His manifestation of the Trinity to us.

And without controversy great is the mystery of godliness: GOD WAS MANIFESTED IN THE

FLESH, justified in the Spirit, seen by angels, preached among the Gentiles, believed on in the world, received up in glory.

-1 Timothy 3:16 | NKJV

6. The Spirit Manifestation

The Spirit of the Lord shall rest upon Him, the Spirit of wisdom and understanding, the Spirit of counsel and might, the Spirit of knowledge and of the fear of the Lord.

-Isaiah 11:2 | NKJV

The Godhead can also manifest themselves into seven different partitions of spirits, and the Godhead can also come together to form one Spirit. Before the throne of the Godhead, there are seven lamps of fire representing the seven spirits of God.

And from the throne proceeded lightnings, thunderings, and voices. SEVEN LAMPS OF FIRE WERE BURNING BEFORE THE THRONE, WHICH ARE THE SEVEN SPIRITS OF GOD.

-Revelation 4:5 | NKJV

The Spirit of wisdom, the Spirit of knowledge, the Spirit of understanding, the Spirit of the fear of the Lord, the Spirit of counsel, the Spirit of might, and the Spirit of Truth were all predetermined as the spirit kind of manifestation that the Godhead decided before Genesis 1:1.

7. The Non-Living Manifestation

NOW THE LORD APPEARED AT THE TABERNACLE IN A PILLAR OF CLOUD, and the pillar of cloud stood above the door of the tabernacle.

-Deuteronomy 31:15 | NKJV

There are many manifestations that the Godhead predetermined before Genesis 1:1. He used non-living things to manifest Himself to us in the past and can use them too to manifest Himself in our present time because He is the same yesterday, today, and forever.

God being the rock of ages, our shield, and Buckler, the Consuming fire, pillar of cloud, pillar of fire, the burning bush and what have you, demonstrate that He can use the weak things, foolish things, and non-living things to confound the wise.

Chapter 7

BEFORE GENESIS 1:1, THE GODHEAD EXISTED AS THREE INDEPENDENT PERSONALITIES

And now, O Father, glorify Me together with Yourself, with the glory which I had with You before the world was.

-John 17:5 | NKJV

*One God, Three Persons

The doctrine of the Trinity means that there is one God who eternally exists as three distinct Persons - the Father, Son, and Holy Spirit. Stated differently, God is one in essence and three in person. These definitions express three crucial truths:

1. The Father, Son, and Holy Spirit are distinct Persons.

2. Each Person of the Godhead is fully God.

3. There is only one God.

The Father, Son, and Holy Spirit are distinct Persons. The Bible speaks of the Father as God (Philippians 1:2), Jesus as God (Titus 2:13), and the Holy Spirit as God (Acts 5:3-4).

Are these just three different ways of looking at God, or simply ways of referring to three different roles that God plays? The answer must be no, because the Bible also shows that the Father, Son, and Holy Spirit are distinct Persons.

For example, since the Father sent the Son into the world (John 3:16), he cannot be the same person as the Son. Likewise, after the Son returned to the Father (John 16:10), the Father and the Son sent the Holy Spirit into the world (John

14:26; Acts 2:33). Therefore, the Holy Spirit must be distinct from the Father and the Son.

In the baptism of Jesus, we saw the Father speaking from heaven and the Spirit descending from heaven as a dove when Jesus Christ came out of the water (Mark 1:10-11). John 1:1 affirms that Jesus is God and at the same time, He was 'with God,' showing that Jesus Christ is a distinct Person from God the Father (see also John 1:18).

And in John 16:13-15, we see that although there is a close unity between the three persons, the Holy Spirit is also distinct from the Father and the Son.

That the Father, Son, and Holy Spirit are distinct Persons means that the Father is not the Son, the Son is not the Holy Spirit, and the Holy Spirit is not the Father. Jesus is God, but he is not the Father or the Holy Spirit. The Holy Spirit is God, but he is not the Son or the Father. They are different Persons, not three different ways of looking at God.

The personhood of each member of the Trinity means that each Person has a distinct centre of consciousness. Thus, they relate to each other personally the Father regards himself as 'I' while he regards the Son and Holy Spirit as 'you.' Likewise, the Son regards himself as 'I,' but the Father and the Holy Spirit as 'you.'

Often it is objected, '*If Jesus is God, then He must have prayed to Himself while He was on earth.*' But the answer to this objection lies in simply applying what we have already seen. While Jesus and the Father are both God, they are different Persons.

Thus, Jesus Christ prayed to God the Father without praying to Himself. In fact, it is precisely the continuing dialogue between the Father and the Son (Matthew 3:17; 17:5;

John 5:19; 11:41-42; 17:1) that furnishes the best evidence that they are distinct Persons with distinct centres of consciousness.

Sometimes the Personhood of the Father and Son is appreciated, but the Personhood of the Holy Spirit is neglected. Sometimes the Spirit is treated more like a 'force' than a Person. But the Holy Spirit is not an 'it,' but a 'He' (see John 14:26; 16:7–15; Acts 8:16).

The fact that the Holy Spirit is a Person, not an impersonal force (like gravity), is also shown by the fact that He speaks (Hebrews 3:7), reasons (Acts 15:28), thinks and understands (1 Corinthians 2:10-11), wills (1 Corinthians 12:11), feels (Ephesians 4:30), and gives personal fellowship (2 Corinthians 13:14). These are all qualities of His personhood.

In addition to these texts, the others we mentioned above clarify that the Personhood of the Holy Spirit is distinct from the Personhood of the Son and the Father. They are three real persons, not three roles God plays.

Another serious error people have made is to think that the Father became the Son, who then became the Holy Spirit. Contrary to this, the passages we have seen imply that God always was and always will be three Persons. There was never a time when one of the Persons of the Godhead did not exist. They are all eternal.

While the three members of the Trinity are distinct, this does not mean that any is inferior to the other. Instead, they are all identical in attributes. They are equal in power, love, mercy, justice, holiness, knowledge, and all other qualities.

Each Person is fully God. If God is three Persons, does this mean that each Person is 'one third' of God? Does the Trinity mean that God is divided into three parts?

The doctrine of the Trinity does not divide God into three parts. The Bible is clear that all three Persons are each one-hundred percent God. The Father, Son, and Holy Spirit are each fully God.

For example, Colossians 2:9 says of Christ, '*in Him all the fullness of deity dwells in bodily form.*' We should not think of God as a 'pie' cut into three pieces, each piece representing a Person. This would make each Person less than fully God and thus not God at all.

Rather, 'the being of each Person is equal to the whole being of God.' The divine essence is not something that is divided between the three persons, but is fully in all three persons without being divided into 'parts.'

Thus, the Son is not one-third of the being of God; He is all of the being of God. The Father is not one-third of the being of God; He is all of the being of God. And likewise, with the Holy Spirit.

Thus, as Wayne Grudem writes, '*When we speak of the Father, Son, and Holy Spirit together we are not speaking of any greater being than when we speak of the Father alone, the Son alone, or the Holy Spirit alone.*'

There is only one God. If each Person of the Trinity is distinct and yet fully God, then should we conclude that there is more than one God? Obviously, we cannot, for Scripture is clear that there is only one God: '*There is no other God besides me, a righteous God and a Saviour; there is none besides me. Turn to me and be saved, all the ends of the earth! For I am God, and there is no other*' (Isaiah 45:21-22; see also Isaiah 44:6-8; Exodus 15:11; Deuteronomy 4:35; 6:4-5; 32:39; 1 Samuel 2:2; 1 Kings 8:60).

Having seen that the Father, the Son, and the Holy Spirit are distinct Persons, that they are each fully God, and that there is nonetheless only one God, we must conclude that all three Persons are the same God. In other words, there is one God who exists as three distinct Persons.

If there is one passage which most clearly brings all of this together, it is Matthew 28:19: '*Make disciples of all the nations, baptizing them in the name of the Father and the Son and the Holy Spirit.*'

First, notice that, the Father, Son, and Holy Spirit are distinguished as distinct Persons. We baptize into the name of the Father and the Son and the Holy Spirit.

Second, notice that each Person must be deity because they are all placed on the same level. In fact, God the Son have us baptized in the name of a mere creature? Surely not. Therefore, each of the Persons into whose name we are to be baptized must be deity.

Third, notice that although the three divine Persons are distinct, we are baptized into their name (singular), and not names (plural). The three Persons are distinct, yet they constitute one name (Jesus Christ). This can only be if they share one essence.

3

---

*Matt Perman. *What Is the Doctrine of the Trinity?* Retrieved from January 23, 2006 from: https://www.desiringgod.org/articles/what-is-the-doctrine-of-the-trinity

Chapter 8

THE COMMON GOAL OF THE GODHEAD BEFORE GENESIS 1:1

Then God said, "LET US make man in Our image, according to Our likeness; let them have dominion over the fish of the sea, over the birds of the air, and over the cattle, over all the earth and over every creeping thing that creeps on the earth."

-Genesis 1:26 | NKJV

Three Persons, One Essence Of Goal

Essence, what does essence mean? As I said earlier, it means the same thing as being. God's essence is His being. To be even more precise, essence is what you are. At the risk of sounding too physical, essence can be understood as the 'stuff' that you 'consist of.'

Of course, we are speaking by analogy here, for we cannot understand this physically about God. 'God is spirit' (John 4:24). Further, we clearly should not think of God as 'comprising' anything other than divinity. The 'substance' of God is God, not a bunch of 'ingredients' that taken together yield deity.

Person, regarding the Trinity, we use the term 'Person' differently than we use it in everyday life. Therefore, it is often difficult to have a concrete definition of Person as we use it with regard to the Trinity.

What we do not mean by Person is an 'independent individual' in the sense that both I and another human are separate, independent individuals who can exist apart from one another.

What we do mean by Person is something that regards himself as 'I' and others as 'You.' So the Father, for example, is a different Person from the Son because He regards the Son as a 'You,' even though He regards Himself as 'I.' Thus, in regards to the Trinity, we can say that 'Person' means a distinct subject which regards himself as an "I" and the other two as a 'You.'

These distinct subjects are not a division within the being of God, but 'a form of personal existence other than a difference in being' (Grudem, 255; I believe that this is a helpful definition, but it should be recognized that Grudem himself is offering this as more of an explanation than definition of Person).

How do they relate? The relationship between essence and Person, then, is as follows. Within God's one, undivided being is an "unfolding" into three personal distinctions. These personal distinctions are modes of existence within the divine being, but are not divisions of the divine being. They are personal forms of existence other than a difference in being.

The late theologian Herman Bavinck has stated something very helpful at this point: '*The persons are modes of existence within the being; the Persons differ among themselves as the one mode of existence differs from the other, and - using a common illustration - as the open palm differs from a fist*' (Bavinck, The Doctrine of God [Banner of Truth Trust, 1991], page 303).

Because each of these 'forms of existence' are relational (and thus are Persons), they are each a distinct centre of consciousness, with each centre of consciousness regarding himself as 'I' and the others as 'you.'

These three Persons all 'comprise' the same 'stuff' (that is, the same 'what' or essence). As theologian and apologist Norman Geisler has explained it, *'while essence is what you are, person is who you are. So, God is one 'what' but three 'who's.'*

The divine essence is thus not something that exists 'above' or 'separate from' the three Persons, but the divine essence is the being of the three Persons. Neither should we think of the Persons as being defined by attributes added on to the being of God. Wayne Grudem explains.....

But if each person is fully God and has all of God's being, then we also should not think that the personal distinctions are any kind of additional attributes added on to the being of God.... Rather, each person of the Trinity has all the attributes of God, and no one Person has any attributes that are not possessed by the others.

We say that the Persons are real, that they are not just different ways of looking at the one being of God... the only way it seems possible to do that distinction between the persons is not a difference of 'being' but a difference of 'relationships.'

This is something far removed from our human experience, where every different human 'person' is a different being as well. Somehow God's being is so much greater than ours that within His one undivided being there can be an unfolding into interpersonal relationships, so there can be three distinct persons.

The Goal Of Salvation

Before the beginning, the Godhead had a plan. They knew what would happen in the times to come. Don't be shocked that, God is aware of tomorrow. He is God but not man. As mortals we are so limited but God is unlimited.

The Godhead knew that the most important beings who needed their arms of salvation is humans. Why? Because they are the only beings who would be created in their image and likeness.

A common vision was set by the Godhead that, anything they do, would all revolve around their goal of saving humans. All other beings could be dealt with, but man would be pardoned.

Not that the Godhead is biased toward their creations, but they would have mercy on them they would have mercy, and would have compassion on whom they would have compassion.

They also knew the people and the angels they would harden for eternal destruction without saving them.

[15]For He says to Moses, "I will have mercy on whomever I will have mercy, and I will have compassion on whomever I will have compassion." [16]So then it is not of him who wills, nor of him who runs, but of God who shows mercy. [17]For the Scripture says to the Pharaoh, "For this very purpose I have raised you up, that I may show My power in you, and that My name may be declared in all the earth." [18]Therefore He has mercy on whom He wills, and whom He wills He hardens.

-Romans 9:15-18 | NKJV

From Genesis to Revelation, it had been the work of God the Father to deliver and save His people from the devil; the work of God the Son to die and use His blood to atone for the sins of the world and bring them to the marvellous light of salvation; the work of the Holy Spirit to seal and help the saints in the path of righteousness and holiness to the destination of the New Jerusalem where they will not fall again for all eternity.

Chapter 9

THE SEPARATION OF POWERS OF THE GODHEAD BEFORE GENESIS 1:1

The Trinitarian Arms Of Government

I always say that the physical things give the impression of what goes on in the spiritual world, and vice versa. Since God creates us in the image of God, His ways of life are sometimes our ways of life and vice versa.

Governance started right before creation. It is not something man brought from nowhere. It has always existed between the Godhead, which they would exercise on the beings they would create.

…..and the GOVERNMENT WILL BE UPON HIS SHOULDER…..

-Isaiah 9:6 | NKJV

This Trinitarian arm of government is likened to the federal governance which has three branches of government which are the Executive, Legislature, and the Judiciary. Let us therefore look at what these mean, and we can liken them to the separation of powers between the Godhead.

How The Earthly Federal Governance Started

In 1787, 11 years after state representatives signed the Declaration of Independence, representatives once again met at the State House in Philadelphia. Fifty-five representatives met over the course of four months in order to draft the United States Constitution. The framers drafted the Constitution to purposely divide governing powers between several administrative branches.

This way, no one branch holds too much power, and each branch holds checks and balances over the others. The framers instituted this system of government hoping it would last into 'remote futurity.' It worked, as we continue to use this system of government today.

Though the earthly federal government started in 1787, the Trinitarian arm of governance started in eternity before Genesis 1:1, long before any mortal or any being existed.

The Executive

The Executive branch is the branch that the President works in, along with the Cabinet departments. It also has independent government agencies.

1. The Executive is the enforcer of law, thus it enforces laws made or enacted by the legislature.

2. The Executive holds the responsibility for the government administrative system.

3. The Executive it has the authority to adjourn and dissolve the legislature.

4. The formulation and execution of governmental policies are also the responsibility of the executive.

5. The Executive directs relations with foreign governments despite of preparing the annual financial reports and proposal of the expenditure and taxes before presenting to the parliament or the legislature for approval.

6. The Executive branch issues regulations to govern the government departments.

7. As the Executive body including all the government servants, it also holds the responsibility for delivering services such as healthcare, welfare, education, finance and what have you, to the people.

8. The Executive body also commands armed forces for the defence and protection of the state security, recommend legislation, and issue ordinances.

The God Of The Executive (President)

You may wonder the particular Godhead who handles this office. Don't worry at all. You will soon discover. In eternity, before creation, one of the Godhead needed to be the President. He needed to be tasked with the implementation of the whole decision made by the Legislature.

The God who was decided upon was called God, the Father. The title 'Father' shows us the head of something. The whole Godhead needed one leader and someone who would serve as the overall Controller of the affairs of the things being created. That was why He was given the title 'Father.'

Since the President is being elected by the citizens, it was the decision of the inner circle to make one of them the God of the Executive and head of the Godhead.

The Twelve Tribes Of Israel, The Cabinet Of God The Father

12"These shall stand on Mount Gerizim to bless the people, when you have crossed over the Jordan: SIMEON, LEVI, JUDAH, ISSACHAR, JOSEPH, and BENJAMIN; 13and these shall stand on Mount Ebal to curse: REUBEN, GAD, ASHER, ZEBULUN, DAN, and NAPHTALI.

-Deuteronomy 27:12-13 | NKJV

Also she had a great and high wall with twelve gates, and twelve angels at the gates, and names written on them, which are the NAMES OF THE TWELVE TRIBES OF THE CHILDREN OF ISRAEL:

-Revelation 21:12 | NKJV

If indeed God the Father is the President of all, then where is His Cabinet? When Apostle John's spirit was being pulled into the head of God to look what was in it and for that matter made him able to write the Book of Revelation, he saw twenty-four elders. Twelve of them were the twelve tribes of Israel.

These elders were not there in heaven for fun. They came to earth to help establish the kingdom of their President, who is Jesus Christ.

The Legislature

Now the wall of the city had twelve foundations, and on them were the NAMES OF THE TWELVE APOSTLES OF THE LAMB.

-Revelation 21:14 | NKJV

1. The Legislature makes law, amends and replaces old laws, it controls, criticise, supervises, and scrutinizes (meneliti) the administration or activities of the executive and influence the policies of the government.

2. The legislature is also the representative for the people. In some country, the legislature sometime holds the judicial function like they can prefer the charge of impeachment on their executives (thus president or vice president).

3. The Legislature also has the power to elect the head of the state, India for example, the lower house and the upper house and the state legislative bodies elect the president.

4. Last, the legislature also controls the national finance, no money could be spent or raised by the executive without the previous consent and approval of the parliament. The power of the legislature includes granting of money for expenses on public services, impose taxes and allowing loans.

The Legislative God (Attorney General)

The Godhead who became responsible for the legislative arm of governance is God the Son. Since this arm of government makes laws, the constitution comprising words and all that, the Word of God as a Person of the Godhead was of no exemption. No one can make any better law without being in the shoes of the people.

When God the Son came on earth, He taught us as One having authority because He was the Word Himself. There was no question the Pharisees asked Him He couldn't answer them.

Even at the year of 12, He was teaching the Popes, Bishops, Apostles, and other distinguished men of God in the temple concerning the things they already knew and what they were ignorant of, for three days without them noticing three days have already elapsed.

You remember the woman who committed adultery and was caught in the very act? This case looked like a dead end as the physical legislative arm of the temple thought for God the Son – but being the Head of all legislation, He beat them at their own game and saved the woman.

Looking at the ministry of God the Son, He amended many constitutions of the Old Testament, which was not there in the Ten Commandments. Even the Ten Commandments that God the Father gave to the Israelites, it was Him, Moses wrote about (John 5:46).

All these things were all evidences of God the Son being the Attorney General over the Legislative branch of governance.

The Parliamentarians

[13]And when it was day, He called His disciples to Himself; and from them He chose twelve whom He also named apostles: [14]SIMON, whom He also named Peter, and ANDREW his brother; JAMES and JOHN; PHILIP and BARTHOLOMEW; [15]MATTHEW and THOMAS; JAMES the son of Alphaeus, and SIMON called the Zealot; [16]JUDAS the son of James, and Judas Iscariot who also became a traitor.

-Luke 6:13-16 | NKJV

Every Legislation needs an Attorney General and His representatives. The representatives are often called the Parliamentarians. The Attorney General we all know is God the Son, but it seems His parliamentarians are quite unknown but not never. The Bible contains all the details we ever need.

When God the Son came into the world, He chose twelve disciples. Judas Iscariot was a fulfilment of His death but substantially not one of His Parliamentarians. Saul who became Paul replaced Judas Iscariot.

The twelve Apostles as the Attoney General's parliamentarians are Peter, James, John, Andrew, Philip, Thomas, Bartholomew, Matthew, James (the son of Alphaeus), Simon Zelotes, Judas (brother of James), and Paul.

These twelve Apostles are part of the twenty-four elders Apostle John saw during the revelation of Jesus Christ. Apostle John was one of the twenty-four elders, yet he didn't know because before you are born, God takes that heavenly identity from your memory. Only One mortal knew who He was in heaven and that is Jesus Christ.

The Judiciary

1. The Judiciary is a branch of government that is concerned with the administration of justice.

2. The Judiciary is the guardian of the constitution. If the laws made by the legislature or the states are conflicted with the constitution, the judiciary could declare the laws as invalid.

3. The Judiciary interprets laws, the constitutions, and the statutes.

4. The Judiciary hears and decides disputes.

5. The Judiciary also makes laws when the existing laws are blurred or confusing or conflicting each other. Sometimes, the Judiciary can determine what law should prevail according to the circumstances and situation.

6. The Judiciary also functions as the advisory body, which it holds the responsibility of giving advices when the government seeks for it.

The God Of The Judiciary (Special Prosecutor)

The Judge who is the head of the Judiciary, is the Spirit of God. Why am I saying this? This is because the Spirit of God is being seen in the new dispensation first of all, prosecuting Ananias and Sapphira when they violated the law of truth, He gave them a capital punishment of death. As a Special Prosecutor, He was interpreting the constitution of lying.

When one stands in the box before the Judge and is found guilty, the Judge doesn't pardon you, but punishes you by sentencing you to prison. That is what the Spirit of God is, and

He has His own way of punishing people who violates the constitution. He can imprison you with all sorts of diseases, infirmities, misfortunes, barrenness, financial difficulties, and all kinds of physical and spiritual problems.

We link every situation with the devil, but do you think a Judge who sentences a culprit is a devil? Absolute Not! It is not every bad thing that is done by the devil. Even the things that the devil does, it is the Lord that grants him the permission (Job 1:12).

The Spirit of God is the only Godhead that doesn't forgive when you sin against Him (Mark 3:28-29). This is because no Judge forgives a culprit, guilty by evidence, and makes him or her go scot free unless he prosecutes the person by fine or by imprisonment.

The Panel Of Judges

And from the throne proceeded lightnings, thunderings, and voices. SEVEN LAMPS OF FIRE were burning before the throne, which are the SEVEN SPIRITS OF GOD.

-Revelation 4:5 | NKJV

In an advanced court such as supreme courts where the law is being interpreted, there is not a single Judge who handles cases. He works with other panel of judges. It is not that the judges cannot take the decisions alone, but teamwork gives a better hearing and judgement.

The panel of judges for the Spirit of God are the seven branches of the Spirit of God. They are: Wisdom, Knowledge, Fear of the Lord, Might, Counsel, Understanding, and Truth (Holy Spirit).

The Lawyers

Before the throne there was a sea of glass, like crystal. And in the midst of the throne, and around the throne, were FOUR LIVING CREATURES full of eyes in front and in back.

-Revelation 4:6 | NKJV

Moses, advising God to stop wiping out the Israelites and using the seed of Moses instead of Abraham, tells us that Moses was not just an ordinary person. He was one lawyer in heaven who plead the case of men even though the Ultimate Lawyer is Jesus Christ – the mediator between God and man.

Judges work with lawyers. Lawyers actually don't cover up the crimes of the culprit by defending them in the court but a professional who is authorised to practise law, conduct lawsuits or give legal advice. In the court of law, they barrage with questions in order to get people to admit something.

The lawyers who work with the Spirit of God are the four living creatures. Look at the vision Ezekiel had on them. Wherever the Spirit of God went, the four living creatures also went.

WHEREVER THE SPIRIT WANTED TO GO, THEY WENT, because there the spirit went; and the wheels were lifted together with them, for the spirit of the living creatures was in the wheels.

-Ezekiel 1:20 | NKJV

The four living creatures are not just creatures, but they were born as humans to live amongst us. If God the Son became a human, the four living creatures are of no exception. Together, their names are AMEN, which entails Abraham, Moses, Elijah, and Noah.

All these arms of government concerning the Godhead made them carry out their division of labour with all separation of powers successfully till now.

BEFORE GENESIS 1:1, THERE WAS NO OTHER GOD BESIDE THE GODHEAD

I am the Alpha and the Omega, the Beginning and the End, the First and the Last."

-Revelation 22:13 | NKJV

All through the Bible, we have come across many verses and chapters that best describe the Godhead as having no other competition. To have someone to be like you shows how co-equal you are or can become. It is a very important thing we need to realise if we want to have a walk with people and also a need of walk of faith with our Maker.

The most important event of all time, known as creation, has made us to understand that the Godhead is in the persons of the Father, Son, and the Holy Spirit as the Only Godhead who formed the universe and all its entirety.

If there had been any other Godhead, they would have spoken or done something for us to determine their existence. Since there was no entity to have risen before creation to declare his or her existence, we can be certain of the triune Godhead as one and only.

Jesus Christ – The Fullness Of The Godhead

For in HIM DWELLS ALL THE FULLNESS OF THE GODHEAD BODILY;

-Colossians 2:9 | NKJV

For us to understand the establishment of the Godhead, we have to look at the man Jesus Christ. His body serving as a temple could house the three Persons of the Godhead – God the Father, God the Son, and God the Holy Spirit.

Many wonder that if Jesus Christ was God, why was He praying and who was He praying to? If Jesus Christ was praying, the body was communicating with the three Persons of God that were in Him.

The body of Jesus Christ was housing all the three Persons of God (Godhead) in Him.

Which is HIS BODY, THE FULLNESS OF HIM WHO FILLS ALL IN ALL.

-Ephesians 1:23 | NKJV

We should note that the Persons of God are not physical entities but spiritual because God is not flesh but Spirit (John 4:24).

Jesus Christ – The New Name For The Godhead

Go therefore and make disciples of all the nations, baptizing them in the NAME OF THE FATHER AND OF THE SON AND OF THE HOLY SPIRIT,

-Matthew 28:19 | NKJV

When the body that the three persons of God were living in was ascending into heaven, He said we should baptise in the name of the Father, Son, and the Holy Spirit. We should note the words carefully. He didn't say names but 'name.'

What is the name was He talking about? Before the three Persons of God could become flesh, they sent angel Gabriel to give the name Jesus to the two parents who would parent the body they would be living in.

²¹And she will bring forth a Son, and you shall call His name JESUS, for He will save His people from their sins. ²⁵And did not know her till she had brought forth her firstborn Son. And he called His name Jesus.

-Matthew 1:21, 25 | NKJV

To confirm this name, the Godhead wanted the Apostles to baptise in, let us look at the name the Apostles used in their baptism after the Holy Spirit came into them.

Then Peter said to them, "Repent, and let every one of you BE BAPTIZED IN THE NAME OF JESUS CHRIST for the remission of sins; and you shall receive the gift of the Holy Spirit.

-Acts 2:38 | NKJV

The three Persons in the Godhead are all having the same name now. We used to know God the Father, God the Son, and God the Holy Spirit, but now it is not so. God the Father, Son, and the Holy Spirit are now called JESUS CHRIST.

40 Reasons Why There Is No Other God Beside Jesus Christ

1. Before Genesis 1:1, the Godhead was established that teaches us about the identity of the one and only True God whose name is Jesus Christ.

I am the Lord, and there is no other; there is no God besides Me. I will gird you, though you have not known Me,

-Isaiah 45:5 | NKJV

There are many gods in the Bible and many gods in our world now, but what distinguishes the Creator from them is because He is one God. There is one God with a capital G identifying Him as the Supreme Being over all gods.

The gods we know can be identified with names and the greatest name above every other name that God can be identified with, is the name Jesus Christ.

2. Before Genesis 1:1, the Godhead was established as a caution to humanity who does not worship Jesus Christ as the one and only True Gid.

"You shall have no other gods before Me.

-Exodus 20:3 | NKJV

Even though there are many gods out there created by God, He does not expect us to worship them. This is because there are adverse consequences awaiting those who take such a decision in Hades temporally and the lake of fire eternally.

Many people ask that if God created palm trees, why does He forbid us not to use them to make alcoholic drink then? It is the same thing applying to gods. God created everything, but He does not want us to prioritize them first in our lives and give it more attention than God.

Today money has become an idol for many believers, and without it they think they can't serve God well. They think they should get money first before starting ministry so they won't beg for bread.

3. Before Genesis 1:1, the Godhead was established for us to know that Jesus Christ is the one and only Jealous God.

(For you shall worship no other god, for the Lord, whose name is Jealous, is a jealous God),

-Exodus 34:14 | NKJV

God is a jealous God, but one of the works of the flesh is jealousy. If God is jealous, why does He want us to refrain from jealousy then? We have two types of jealousy: *godly jealousy* and *ungodly jealousy*.

Godly jealousy is the vigilance of guarding someone from being disposed to Satan, who is the rival of God. It is what God cannot tolerate when you are becoming unfaithful to Him through sin. *Godly jealousy leads to salvation.*

Ungodly jealousy is more or less like envy, which is the hostility toward a rival or one believed to enjoy an advantage over another. *Ungodly jealousy leads to sin and evil.*

When there is presence of godly jealousy, then, there is also a proof of godly love. There cannot be godly jealousy without love. When God is not jealous when you sin, then you are not part of His children.

It is because God loves us as His children that is why He is suspicious or fearful of being displaced by the rival who is Satan. Before Genesis 1:1, the Godhead as one having no rival beside them, was a clear sign that God would be a Jealous God some time to come.

4. Before Genesis 1:1, the Godhead was established to exhibit the sovereignty of the one True God whose name is Jesus Christ.

Then Hezekiah prayed before the Lord, and said: "O Lord God of Israel, the One who dwells between the cherubim, You are God, You alone, of all the kingdoms of the earth. You have made heaven and earth.

-2 Kings 19:15 | NKJV

The oneness of the Godhead shows that there is none like our God – Jesus Christ. If we are to rate two things at a time, definitely, one will be rated above the other and the more rated one will have none beside it in terms of greatest rating.

The reason God is King of all Kings and Lord of all Lords is that there is none beside Him in terms of sovereignty. If someone thinks he or she is great in status, authority or power, then there is a God above him or her.

If we ever need power, authority, or status or any kind of leadership, we can't go behind the only God who is sovereign over all. Before Genesis 1:1, God knew men would struggle if they cast Him aside when they want power because He is the only Powerful one and all other powers bow down to Him.

5. Before Genesis 1:1, the Godhead was established for us to know that Jesus Christ is the one and only True God who is the greatest of all.

For You are great, and do wondrous things; You alone are God.

-Psalms 86:10 | NKJV

There have been many great people who have left an indelible ink in the history of the world, but there has not been anyone who can surpass the greatness of God. The greatness of the Godhead depicts their humility.

God – the greatest of all things and people, became the humblest of all. God, the greatest of all, became humble enough to enter the womb of a woman. Despite His greatness, He became humble to pass through the birth canal of a woman.

He was born in the humblest place in a manger where sheep were kept. The greatest of all became a baby to be breastfed.

The greatest of all wisdom was taught how to speak, walk, eat, do construction work and what have you.

In His ministry, He was so humble that He ate with sinners and mingled with children. The greatest of all humbled Himself to the point that He didn't have a place to lay His head, yet, heaven was His residence and the earth was His footstool.

Greatness is now seen in arrogance concerning humanity, but in humility concerning Godliness. *The humblest person is the greatest person.* If we think we are great, then we need to have the mentality of humility. Before Genesis 1:1, this was what the Godhead wanted us to learn.

6. Before Genesis 1:1, the Godhead was established for us to know that there is no kingdom that can surpass the kingdom of Jesus Christ.

"O Lord of hosts, God of Israel, the One who dwells between the cherubim, You are God, You alone, of all the kingdoms of the earth. You have made heaven and earth.

-Isaiah 37:16 | NKJV

Royalty is seen in the blood that one can be related to. There is no royalty than the blood of the Godhead (Jesus Christ). From Genesis to Revelation, no one can become a child of God without relating to the blood of Jesus Christ.

There is no blood that can speak better things than the blood of Jesus Christ. There is no blood that can wash the sins of men than the blood of Jesus Christ. There is no royal life than the life of righteousness, holiness, and sanctification.

When you have covenant with the blood of Jesus Christ, you have access to unlimited riches of God in His kingdom. You become heirs with God and joint-heirs with Jesus Christ.

Before Genesis 1:1, there was no other royal kingdom anywhere apart from the royalty of God. If there is any kingdom in the world, it proceeded from the kingdom of God, and it is Him who gives utterances of royalty.

For the kingdom is the Lord's, and He rules over the nations.

-Psalms 22:28 | NKJV

But you are a chosen generation, a royal priesthood, a holy nation, His own special people, that you may proclaim the praises of Him who called you out of darkness into His marvelous light;

-1 Peter 2:9 | NKJV

7. Before Genesis 1:1, the Godhead was established that teaches us that Jesus Christ is the only God who saves.

Now therefore, O Lord our God, save us from his hand, that all the kingdoms of the earth may know that You are the Lord, You alone."

-Isaiah 37:20 | NKJV

There is no other god beside Jesus Christ who can give us salvation for our souls. There is no other way, no other life, and no other truth can save us from our sins.

Many people want salvation from evil around the world which includes diseases, poverty, barrenness, unemployment, starvation, political instability, and many more. *But the greatest enemy that we should seek salvation from, is sin.*

There is only one God who provides us salvation from sin. Because of sin, He had to come down from heaven (His dwelling place as a God) and took upon Himself the form of humanity so He would save us from our sins.

The sins that He was about to rescue us from had a certain penalty, and the only penalty was blood. Because He loved us so much, He paid the penalty with His own blood and died on a cross (as a symbol of the world – north, south, east, and west representing globe).

There is no god who was ready to do this for us but the only God of the Bible named Jesus Christ, paid the penalty with His own blood and saved us from the greatest enemy. If you want salvation, He is ever ready to give it to you as a gift.

Before Genesis 1:1, the Godhead was ever ready to deal with the greatest enemy of humanity, and they were willing to pay the ransom for the remission of our sins.

8. Before Genesis 1:1, the Godhead was established for us to know that Jesus Christ is the one and only true God.

> **That they may know that You, whose name alone is the Lord, are the Most High over all the earth.**
> **-Psalms 83:18 | NKJV**

There is only one God we should know and know Him well. It is Him alone who holds the truth to all knowledge. We may perceive we know certain things, but they may not be the truth. We may know facts, but those facts may not be the truth.

Even if we have the grasp of certain information at our disposal, we only know in part and not all. There is hidden knowledge that is all stored up in one and only God. If we serve Him, He will unravel such secrets to us.

Before Genesis 1:1, He kept such information from us but has revealed them in His Book called the Bible. We can know Him through His Word. Even though we have such information before us, it only takes Him to explain the meaning of what is written in it.

If we ever need wisdom to apply the knowledge, we have in Him the Spirit of wisdom. There is no wiser angel, human or animal than the one and only true God. His understanding concerning knowledge is also infinite. *His foolishness is wiser than the wisest person.*

Because the foolishness of God is wiser than men, and the weakness of God is stronger than men.

-1 Corinthians 1:25 | NKJV

9. Before Genesis 1:1, the Godhead was established for us to know that Jesus Christ is the one and only true Creator.

You alone are the Lord; You have made heaven, the heaven of heavens, with all their host, the earth and everything on it, the seas and all that is in them, and You preserve them all. The host of heaven worships You.

-Nehemiah 9:6 | NKJV

If all things were created through the Word and for Him and in the beginning this same Word was there, was with God, became flesh and lived among us, then this same Word who is God is the Creator called Jesus Christ.

FOR BY HIM ALL THINGS WERE CREATED THAT ARE IN HEAVEN AND THAT ARE ON EARTH, VISIBLE AND INVISIBLE, WHETHER THRONES OR DOMINIONS OR PRINCIPALITIES OR POWERS. ALL THINGS WERE CREATED THROUGH HIM and for Him.

-Colossians 1:16 | NKJV

Many believers are serving God, but they don't know the God they are serving. Many believers believe Jesus Christ is the Son of God and not the One and Only True God. They know the Creator as God, but they don't believe the Word is that Creator.

When Jesus Christ was about to heal one blind man, He demonstrated that He was the Creator of all the universe. He took some mud (dust used to create humanity in Genesis 2:7) and mixed it with His saliva (representing the Word of God in Genesis 1:3) and told him to go to the pool of Siloam (which is by interpretation, sent – representing the sent Spirit that hovered upon the face of the deep in Genesis 1:2).

If the Word was there before Genesis 1:1, then Jesus Christ, who is the same as God is that Creator of all heavens and earth (Genesis 1:1).

10. Before Genesis 1:1, the Godhead was established to depict the universal dominion of Jesus Christ.

Now therefore, O Lord our God, I pray, save us from his hand, that all the kingdoms of the earth may know that You are the Lord God, You alone."
-2 Kings 19:18 NKJV

Jesus Christ has dominion over all whether or not you believe His existence. Jesus Christ is the God of all Atheists and Christians. It is His breath that gives everyone life and He provides for those who are His lovers and enemies.

Even though He has all the power to dominate in heaven, on earth, and under the earth (Matthew 28:18), He doesn't force Himself on His creations to worship Him. Because of His love, He has given us our free will to decide to accept or reject His dominance (Revelation 3:20).

Before Genesis 1:1, the dominion of Jesus Christ was established to exist from everlasting to everlasting and to rule over all creations. It is because of His universal dominion that He judges all creations and determines their eternal residence.

11. Before Genesis 1:1, the Godhead was established for us to place our confidence in Jesus Christ as the one and only true God.

Do not fear, nor be afraid; Have I not told you from that time, and declared it? You are My witnesses. Is there a God besides Me? Indeed there is no other Rock; I know not one.' "

-Isaiah 44:8 | NKJV

Many people place their confidence in people and things because they believe in their abilities, which gives them the freedom from any doubt. They have a certain state of hopefulness that events will be favourable for them.

Confidence is a secret that is confided or entrusted to another. The actions of people are usually based on the hidden things they confine themselves in which other people may not know.

Jesus Christ wants us to have a trustful relationship with Him. People and the things we place our confidence in, have disappointed or failed us before but we can't have faith in Jesus Christ and receive the feedback of failure.

Before Genesis 1:1, Jesus Christ already existed as our Trusted God. All His promises are yes and Amen, freeing us from any doubt when we place our confidence in Him. His Word of promise can never pass away without fulfilment.

12. Before Genesis 1:1, the Godhead was established to depict Jesus Christ as the only dependable God.

"For who is God, except the Lord? and who is a rock, except our God?

-2 Samuel 22:32 | NKJV

Mountains comprise land mass of rocks that project well above their surroundings. Mountains cannot be moved because of its level of dependency. Jesus Christ is the rock of ages who is forever steadfast and sure.

Before Genesis 1:1, Jesus Christ was there, today He is here and tomorrow He will be there for us.

Jesus Christ is the same yesterday, today, and forever.

-Hebrews 13:7 | NKJV

He doesn't sleep nor slumbers and He can never die. If you have anyone worthy of reliance, then it is Jesus Christ because He is consistent with His performance.

13. Before Genesis 1:1, the Godhead was established to show us that Jesus Christ is the Lord of all.

FOR WHO IS GOD, EXCEPT THE LORD? and who is a rock, except our God?

-Psalms 18:31 | NKJV

Jesus Christ is not only a God who needs to be worshipped, but the One who owns everything both visible and invisible. He is not just a Creator, but the Owner. He is so humble to the point that He doesn't brag about the things He owns.

Thomas used to doubt the Lordship of Jesus Christ until He rose from the dead. Thomas - the most doubting figure in the Bible testified that Jesus Christ is indeed Lord over everything, even death.

And Thomas answered and said to Him, "MY LORD and my God!"

-John 20:28 | NKJV

Before Genesis 1:1, everything that was the possession of God was all in Him. Until He created them, He was Lord over all of them in Him. He created all things so He could be Lord over them and to give them to everyone who loves Him.

For by Him all things were created that are in heaven and that are on earth, visible and invisible, whether thrones or dominions or principalities or powers. ALL THINGS were created through Him and FOR HIM.

-Colossians 1:16 | NKJV

14. Before Genesis 1:1, the Godhead was established to give us the location where we can find Jesus Christ.

Thus says the LORD: "the labor of Egypt and merchandise of Cush and of the Sabeans, men of stature, shall come over to you, and they shall be yours; they shall walk behind you, they shall come over in chains; and they shall bow down to you. They will make supplication to you, saying, SURELY GOD IS IN YOU, and there is no other; there is no other God.' "

-Isaiah 45:14 | NKJV

There are many places we can find Jesus Christ. We can find Him in heaven. We can find Him in the temple, thus the body of saints. We can find Jesus Christ in His secret place. He is the Word, and we can also find Him in the Bible.

Before Genesis 1:1, even though Jesus Christ dwelt in the location of approachable light, He made His location readily accessible to us when He came on earth and lived among us.

He is always available to everyone who seeks Him wholeheartedly.

15. Before Genesis 1:1, the Godhead was established to teach us the main agenda why Jesus Christ created the universe.

> **For thus says the Lord, who created the heavens, who is God, who formed the earth and made it, who has established it, who did not create it in vain, who formed it to be inhabited: "I am the Lord, and there is no other.**
>
> **-Isaiah 45:18 | NKJV**

No innovation is ever done without any underlying reason behind it. Being said, the universe was created by God to serve a certain purpose. He didn't create the universe as a false pride or to have any exaggerated sense of self-importance.

He created the universe and everything within it to be productive for success. He blessed animals to be successful and He also blessed humanity to be successful in dominion concerning the things He had created.

As creations of God, we were never created in vain but for us to serve His purpose. Let us therefore find that purpose for which we were created and our existence on earth will be very beneficial in the hereafter.

16. Before Genesis 1:1, the Godhead was established for us to realise that the ultimate taker of lives is Jesus Christ.

> **'Now see that I, even I, am He, and there is no God besides Me; I kill and I make alive; I wound and I heal; nor is there any who can deliver from My hand.**
>
> **-Deuteronomy 32:39 | NKJV**

We can decide to take our own lives; we can be influenced by evil spirits to take our own lives or that of others, and we can die when our time is due, but all these points us to God who created death to bring that physical separation of the soul from the body.

If Before Genesis 1:1, Jesus Christ wrote all the names of the people He would save or those who would not die eternally, then it is telling us that, He also decided those who would die eternally too.

If eternal death is superior than physical death, for which we must fear the One who does that, then we should know that Jesus Christ is the One who takes our lives physically too.

17. Before Genesis 1:1, the Godhead was established for us to know that Jesus Christ is the Only King of all Kings.

"Thus says the Lord, the King of Israel, and his Redeemer, the Lord of hosts: I am the First and I am the Last; besides Me there is no God.

-Isaiah 44:6 | NKJV

There is one and only ultimate President or King over all the heavens, earth and under it whose name is Jesus Christ. He is not just a King, but the King of all Kings. He is the one who appoints kings to rule over the face of the earth.

There is no king or leader who can operate without the utterance of Jesus Christ. This is the reason we have to honour those in authorities in the Lord because it is Jesus Christ who is ruling us through such people.

Let every soul be subject to the governing authorities. For there is no authority except from God, and the authorities that exist are appointed by God.

-Romans 13:1 | NKJV

Jesus Christ is the King of all Kings because before Genesis 1:1, there was no King whose kingdom was established before Him. Jesus Christ has even set a day that all kings will stand before Him to be judged and those who pass the judgement will reign with Him in the everlasting kingdom.

And the nations of those who are saved shall walk in its light, and the kings of the earth bring their glory and honor into it.

-Revelation 21:24 | NKJV

18. Before Genesis 1:1, the Godhead was established to show us that the best Counsellor we can seek advice from is Jesus Christ.

Tell and bring forth your case; yes, let them take counsel together. Who has declared this from ancient time? Who has told it from that time? Have not I, the Lord? And there is no other God besides Me, a just God and a Savior; there is none besides Me.

-Isaiah 45:21 | NKJV

If you ever need someone whose words can guide you in your Godliness, ministry, health, business, marriage, family, social life, and what have you, you can't turn your back on the words of Jesus Christ.

There are many marriage counsellors out there whose marriages are not working, yet they seem happy on the outside, but on the inside; they are hurting. They give expert advices for others but they don't practise what they counsel.

It is like many Ministers of today who preach for others to repent, but they are sinners secretly. They are signboards directing others to New Jerusalem, but they are heading straight to the lake of fire.

Before Genesis 1:1, Jesus Christ was ever ready to be born among us, so His name would be called Counsellor. He knows the answers to all questions, and He proved that when the Jews asked him the toughest questions.

For unto us a Child is born, unto us a Son is given; and the government will be upon His shoulder. And His name will be called Wonderful, COUNSELOR, Mighty God, Everlasting Father, Prince of Peace.

-Isaiah 9:6 | NKJV

19. Before Genesis 1:1, the Godhead was established to depict Jesus Christ as the Only God who is unchangeable.

That they may know from the rising of the sun to its setting that there is none besides Me. I am the Lord, and there is no other;

-Isaiah 45:6 | NKJV

There is a saying that, when the world changes, you must also change as a believer. There are so many Ministers who started well in Ministry as holy people and they preached and taught so. But as time went on, they deviated from what they used to be and what they used to preach and teach.

The God who made one wife and one husband has not changed to permit polygamy. The God who rained fire and brimstone from heaven to destroy Sodom and Gomorrah has not changed to allow homosexuality.

He is holy and there is no way He is ever going to change. If we want to serve Jesus Christ, then we need to be steadfast in our walk of holiness with Him. His holiness is not going to change to conform to the changing trends of Satan, who is the world.

Before Genesis 1:1, God knew He had to set the example of unchangeability so His children would learn from Him and be steadfast in all holiness.

And LET US NOT GROW WEARY WHILE DOING GOOD, for in due season we shall reap if we do not lose heart.

-Galatians 6:9 | NKJV

20. Before Genesis 1:1, the Godhead was established to show us how outstanding Jesus Christ is.

Therefore You are great, O Lord God. For there is none like You, nor is there any God besides You, according to all that we have heard with our ears.

-2 Samuel 7:22 | NKJV

The God who was there before Genesis 1:1, is one and only God we have to serve. He stands tall among all other gods, and there is no one He can ever be compared to. His Godhead is with distinction from the beginning to the end of the world.

Jesus Christ is distinguished from any angel, human, or any animal. Nothing can ever be used to describe Him. He is distinguished from others in all excellence, and He is of major significance or importance than anyone.

The miracles Jesus Christ proved how outstanding He was as a God in human flesh. His outstanding Godhead was proved when He walked on the sea, delivered people from demons, transfigured on the mount, resurrected from the dead after laying down His own life.

21. Before Genesis 1:1, the Godhead was established to show how unapproachable Jesus Christ is.

For since the beginning of the world men have not heard nor perceived by the ear, nor has the eye seen any God besides You, who acts for the one who waits for Him.

-Isaiah 64:4 | NKJV

Even though Jesus Christ can be located, yet He is unapproachable to sinners who are not ready to repent. The Pharisees, Scribes, Sadducees and other Jews who were not ready to repent, couldn't approach who Jesus Christ was in terms of His identity.

Many knew Him to be one of the Prophets. Many knew Him as the carpenter's son. Many knew Him as Beelzebub. Many knew Him as a blasphemer. Many knew Him as a Nazarene, but they didn't know Him as the One and Only True Living God.

Till date, many people can't approach who Jesus Christ is, especially believers. Many people approach Him as the Son of God, but they can't approach Him as the One and Only True Living God. Before Genesis 1:1, He had already predetermined the people who could approach His reality.

22. Before Genesis 1:1, the Godhead was established to portray the exceptionality of Jesus Christ.

To you it was shown, that you might know that the Lord Himself is God; there is none other besides Him.

-Deuteronomy 4:35 | NKJV

Jesus Christ is far beyond what is usual in magnitude or degree. Jesus Christ surpasses what is common or usual or expected. His Godhead deviates widely from the norm of the physical or mental ability.

The teachings of Jesus Christ were so exceptional to the point that, He taught as One who had authority and not as the other Ministers of Israel did. Without the Holy Spirit, you cannot grasp the exceptionality of Jesus Christ.

To grasp the exceptionality of Jesus Christ, is to grasp His words because He is the Word. You cannot fully comprehend who Jesus Christ is, if there is any darkness in you.

23. Before Genesis 1:1, the Godhead was established to show us that Jesus Christ is the most important Person who needs to be considered and imitated more than any other thing.

> **Therefore know this day, and consider it in your heart, that the Lord Himself is God in heaven above and on the earth beneath; there is no other.**
> **-Deuteronomy 4:39 | NKJV**

Knowing Jesus Christ as the One and Only True Living God is carefully studying Him very well in what He did and what He said. Jesus Christ is the Perfect Role Model who has no limitation or shortcomings.

There are many believers who have their Apostles, Prophets, Evangelists, Pastors, and Teachers whom they have as their role models, and they quote 1 Corinthians 11:1 to back such action.

Indeed, we need to imitate Paul, but who did Paul also imitate then? If Paul imitated Jesus Christ, then Jesus Christ is the Perfect Person who needs to be imitated by us.

> **Imitate me, just as I ALSO IMITATE CHRIST.**
> **-1 Corinthians 11:1 | NKJV**

For those believers who even quote 1 Corinthians 11:1, don't even imitate the good lifestyles of Ministers, but their evil lifestyles. Some believers even have worldly celebrities as their role models.

Before Genesis 1:1, Jesus Christ was set as an open spectacle for us as the best role model we should imitate. Cast aside all worldly celebrities and look onto Jesus Christ as your Role Model, because He is the Author and Finisher of your faith who never sinned.

24. Before Genesis 1:1, the Godhead was established for all peoples to know that there is an existence of a God.

That all the peoples of the earth may know that the Lord is God; there is no other.

-1 Kings 8:60 | NKJV

Many people who do not believe in the existence of God anymore once believed in His existence. There is no false or counterfeit thing without the original or the true one that had not already been established.

The creations point to the Creator, but many people after realizing there is a God who created all things, don't want to give glory to Him as the God of their lives. You not liking LG's products, doesn't mean there is no manufacturer called LG.

[20]For since the creation of the world His invisible attributes are clearly seen, being understood by the things that are made, even His eternal power and Godhead, so that they are without excuse, [21]because, although they knew God, they did not glorify Him as God, nor were thankful, but became futile in their thoughts, and their foolish hearts were darkened.

-Romans 1:20-21 | NKJV

You not accepting there is a God, does not mean He is not there. Your belief or unbelief cannot nullify His existence. Many people didn't know there was a God until He came on earth as Jesus Christ.

Before Genesis 1:1, He thought of revealing Himself to the living as the Son of man and to the dead as such. Also, He reveals His existence to us through His Word, so no one can ever find any excuse not to believe He is not there.

And this gospel of the kingdom will be preached in all the world as a witness to all the nations, and then the end will come.
-Matthew 24:14 | NKJV

25. Before Genesis 1:1, the Godhead was established to stir up the faith and hope of Jesus Christ in our lives.

"Look to Me, and be saved, all you ends of the earth! For I am God, and there is no other.
-Isaiah 45:22 | NKJV

Before Genesis 1:1, Jesus Christ, as the One and Only True God, was established for us to place all our faith and hope in Him. He is not a man who can lie, and He is a man who can deceive us.

He is the One who owns everything, and He is capable of providing everything we need and want. We should place our faith and hope in Him because He is not limited concerning the things He can provide for us.

If you ask anything in My name, I will do it.
-John 14:14 | NKJV

Even though God can provide us with the things we need and want, that should not be the reason we must have faith and hope in Jesus Christ. We should have hope and faith in Him because of love and not because of opportunism.

26. Before Genesis 1:1, the Godhead was established for us to always remember Jesus Christ concerning His ways of old.

Remember the former things of old, for I am God, and there is no other; I am God, and there is none like Me,

-Isaiah 46:9 | NKJV

Before Genesis 1:1, Jesus Christ was the old way, the old truth and the old life. He hasn't changed his narrow way of truth and life, and He is not going to create any other way, not as Satan always creates alternative ways to deceive.

Because men are prone to deceit, have short memory, and sometimes forget the things Jesus Christ has already done for them, that is why He always wants us to meditate upon His Word day and night to keep us in the remembrance of His Word.

27. Before Genesis 1:1, the Godhead was established for us to have the blessing of realising Jesus Christ as the One and Only True Living God.

And he returned to the man of God, he and all his aides, and came and stood before him; and he said, "Indeed, now I know that there is no God in all the earth, except in Israel; now therefore, please take a gift from your servant."

-2 Kings 5:15 | NKJV

Before Genesis 1:1, those whose names were written in the Lamb's (Jesus Christ) Book of life are blessed and these people hear the voice of the Shepherd and believe in Him as their one and only True living God.

You can never be a blessed person without realizing that Jesus Christ is the true living God. *Blessing is not about the possession of material things, but the possession of the knowledge of spiritual things that comes from Jesus Christ.*

One of such blessings is the knowledge of Jesus Christ as the one and only true living God. There are many people whom such knowledge is hidden from them and others who are taught too, cannot understand unless they are also the sheep of Jesus Christ.

28. Before Genesis 1:1, the establishment of the lonesomeness of the Godhead of Jesus Christ, didn't nullify the existence of idols.

Therefore concerning the eating of things offered to idols, we know that an idol is nothing in the world, and that there is no other God but one.

-1 Corinthians 8:4 | NKJV

There is only one God named Jesus Christ, but why is there the presence of other gods then? This question is just like asking why were there many good trees in the Garden of Eden and yet God placed the forbidden fruit there?

God created good things, but He gave free will to His creations. The angels rebelled, and some became gods who demanded worship contrary to the worship of the one and only true Living God whose name is called Jesus Christ.

The presence of good things does not nullify the presence of evil things, and vice versa. The fact that there are false Ministers out there doesn't nullify the presence of true Ministers of God.

If indeed there is the presence of many gods out there who are false, then indeed, there must be a true God. Jesus Christ is the head over all gods and all things, and it is Him alone we must worship.

And he is the head of the body, the church: who is the beginning, the firstborn from the dead; that in all things he might have the preeminence.

-Colossians 1:18 | NKJV

29. Before Genesis 1:1, the Godhead was established for us to give honour to Jesus Christ, who is the One and only true living God.

How can you believe, who receive honor from one another, and do not seek the honor that comes from the only God?

-John 5:43 | NKJV

Before Genesis 1:1, it pleased the Godhead that, in Jesus Christ should all the fullness of the Godhead (Father, Son, and Holy Spirit) be. It is Jesus Christ alone that we should all honour because He is the only God who died and saved us from our sins.

Now to the King eternal, immortal, invisible, to God who alone is wise, be HONOR and glory forever and ever. Amen.

-1 Timothy 1:17 | NKJV

If we truly honour Jesus Christ, it will be seen in our thoughts and actions. We will never live contrary to the commandments of Jesus Christ, but will obey Him as such.

30. Before Genesis 1:1, the Godhead was established for us to know that Jesus Christ is the only God who is eternal.

Now to the King ETERNAL, immortal, invisible, to God who alone is wise, be honor and glory forever and ever. Amen.

-1 Timothy 1:17 | NKJV

Jesus Christ told the Samaritan woman that He is the only One who can give us the living water. He again told us that He is the life and because He is life, even His words are not dead words but are filled with life. Jesus Christ is the only eternal God.

If we believe and accept Him into our lives, we will also have the gift of eternal life. It is better to leave any religion that does not believe in Jesus Christ and come into Christianity so you can have eternal life for your soul.

31. Before Genesis 1:1, the Godhead was established to depict Jesus Christ as the one and only God who is the Truth.

So the scribe said to Him, "Well said, Teacher. You have spoken the truth, for there is one God, and there is no other but He.

-Mark 12:32 | NKJV

What sets Jesus Christ apart from all other gods is because He is the only God who knows the truth, lives by it and tells it. All other gods are liars! If they know the truth, they would have let their worshippers know that Jesus Christ is the one and only God they need to worship and not them.

Many people don't like the truth because they know their ways are deceitful. In that case, they will like to mingle with people who will not 'hurt' them with the truth they know. But it is better to be hurt with the truth than to be loved with lies.

Before Genesis 1:1, Jesus Christ knew the people who would readily accept Him as their God of truth and people who would accept Satan as their god of lies.

32. Before Genesis 1:1, the Godhead was established to show us that there can be no other god who has ever existed, is existing and will ever exist for all time than Jesus Christ.

"You are My witnesses," says the Lord, "And My servant whom I have chosen, that you may know and believe Me, and understand that I am He. Before Me there was no God formed, nor shall there be after Me.

-Isaiah 43:10 | NKJV

Before Genesis 1:1, if there was any other god who existed before Jesus Christ, was existing with Him or will exist after Him, then the Bible would have said it. But in Genesis 1:1, we saw that there was only one God who existed as the Creator of heavens and the earth.

We have to know the God we serve and we need to know His name. Many have faith in Jesus Christ but they still believe that there is another God beside Him. There is no other God beside Jesus Christ. The Father, Son, and Holy Spirit is One God and not three Gods.

33. Before Genesis 1:1, the Godhead was established to show the nativeness of the one and only true God whose name is Jesus Christ.

"Yet I am the Lord your God ever since the land of Egypt, and you shall know no God but Me; for there is no savior besides Me.

-Hosea 13:4 | NKJV

Nativeness is the quality of belonging to or being connected with a certain place or region by virtue of birth or origin. Jesus Christ, coming purposely for the lost souls of Israel tells us that He is the same God who took the Jews as His nation.

The birth of Jesus Christ was linked with Abraham and King David, typifying that His nativeness was Israel. But He later came to build Christianity as a nation that can join both Israelites and non-Israelites (Gentiles) together.

Before Genesis 1:1, Jesus Christ was not only willing to connect with one nation called Israel, but He set a time that He would draw all men to Himself through the nation called Christianity.

34. Before Genesis 1:1, the Godhead was established for us to know that when we serve Jesus Christ we will never be put to shame.

> **Then you shall know that I am in the midst of Israel: I am the Lord your God and there is no other. My people shall never be put to shame.**
>
> **-Joel 2:27 | NKJV**

The greatest shame is to be in Hell (temporal place for the souls of sinners after physical death) and lake of fire (permanent place for the souls of sinners as the second death).

King David said in Psalms 37:25 that he was once young and now old, yet he had not seen the righteous forsaken or their children begging for bread. It is a shameful thing to beg.

When you serve Jesus Christ, you won't worry thinking about material things because He will definitely provide. Before Genesis 1:1, He planned of creating everything man would ever need, before creating him.

35. Before Genesis 1:1, the Godhead was established for us to know that Jesus Christ, who needs to be worshipped, is not subject to death.

Now to the King eternal, IMMORTAL, invisible, to God who alone is wise, be honor and glory forever and ever. Amen.

-1 Timothy 1:17 | NKJV

It looked as if death separated the Spirit Jesus Christ had from the body He was in, but it was not so. Before Genesis 1:1, Jesus Christ was an Immortal God who couldn't be subjected to death because the Creator cannot be subjected to the creation.

It was Jesus Christ who laid down His own life and took it again. It was not death who laid His Spirit down for Him or separated His Spirit from His body. The Spirit that was in the body of Jesus Christ was what is called 'the father,' and when He was laying it down, He termed it as 'forsaken.'

And about the ninth hour Jesus cried out with a loud voice, saying, "Eli, Eli, lama sabachthani?" that is, "My God, My God, WHY HAVE YOU FORSAKEN ME?"

-Matthew 27:46 | NKJV

'Forsaken' because the Spirit that the body of Jesus Christ was counting on to live physically, was leaving the body. Because Jesus Christ was immortal, He rose from the dead by Himself after three days.

⁵But the angel answered and said to the women, "Do not be afraid, for I know that you seek Jesus who was crucified. ⁶HE IS NOT HERE; FOR HE IS RISEN, as He said. Come, see the place where the Lord lay.

-Matthew 28:5-6 | NKJV

36. Before Genesis 1:1, the Godhead was established to show us that Jesus Christ is the one and only true God who is wise.

Now to the King eternal, immortal, invisible, to God who alone is WISE, be honor and glory forever and ever. Amen.

-1 Timothy 1:17 | NKJV

If the Creator of the universe is not wise, how could He create such a complex universe then? Sometimes when I think through the creations of Jesus Christ, I become so astonished. The application of knowledge depicts how wise you are.

Many people have knowledge, but they can't convert it into a tangible and meaningful outcome that can bring about benefit and not harm. Jesus Christ had the beneficial wisdom that was displayed in Genesis chapter 1.

He knows what to do at any given point in time. His knowledge is not for cognition, but for application. That is why we have to be the doers of the Word of God and not just the hearers (James 1:22).

Because Jesus Christ is the source of all wisdom, anyone who lacks wisdom can ask from Him and He will provide.

If any of you lacks wisdom, let him ask of God, who gives to all liberally and without reproach, and it will be given to him.

-James 1:5 | NKJV

If King Solomon is the wisest mortal who has ever lived, he acquired it from Jesus Christ.

37. Before Genesis 1:1, the Godhead was established for us to know that all glory belongs to Jesus Christ.

Now to the King eternal, immortal, invisible, to God who alone is wise, be honor and GLORY forever and ever. Amen.

-1 Timothy 1:17 | NKJV

The glory of Jesus Christ as the One and Only True God cannot be approached. Apostle Paul can testify to the fact that he couldn't stand the glory of Jesus Christ on his way to Damascus, and Moses couldn't stand the glory of Jesus Christ either.

Even when Jesus Christ became a man, His state of high honour and brilliant radiant beauty was shown through the things He did and most especially, on the mount of transfiguration.

And He was transfigured before them. His face shone like the sun, and His clothes became as white as the light.

-Matthew 17:2 | NKJV

If we serve Him well, one day we will also have the glory of a transformed body for our souls. We will shine like the brightness of the firmament and as stars forever.

Before Genesis 1:1, the glory of Jesus Christ was kept until the appointed time of His second coming when all eyes will behold it.

38. Before Genesis 1:1, the Godhead was established for us to know that Jesus Christ is the Mighty God.

For unto us a Child is born, unto us a Son is given; and the government will be upon His shoulder. And His name will be called Wonderful, Counselor,

MIGHTY GOD, Everlasting Father, Prince of Peace.

-Isaiah 9:6 | NKJV

All strength belongs to Jesus Christ. Before Genesis 1:1, no one was there to help Him create the heavens, the earth, and its fullness that required the strength of many people.

If Samson was physically stronger, it was Jesus Christ who gave him that might. If there is any other god out there who thinks he is mighty, then that might come from Jesus Christ because it was Him who created them.

Nothing is impossible for Jesus Christ to do because His power is capable of accomplishing everything. Before Genesis, He knew those He would give His strength to.

39. Before Genesis 1:1, the Godhead was established for us to know that Jesus Christ is the Everlasting Father.

For unto us a Child is born, unto us a Son is given; and the government will be upon His shoulder. And His name will be called Wonderful, Counselor, Mighty God, EVERLASTING FATHER, Prince of Peace.

-Isaiah 9:6 | NKJV

Many people know that the Father is a separate God from Jesus Christ, but they don't know Jesus Christ is the same as Everlasting father. When the disciples wanted Jesus Christ to show them the Father, He said they had seen Him already.

[9]Jesus said to him, "Have I been with you so long, and yet you have not known Me, Philip? He who has seen Me has seen the Father; so how can you say, 'Show us the Father'? [10]Do you not believe that I am in the Father, and the Father in Me? The words that

I speak to you I do not speak on My own authority; but the Father who dwells in Me does the works. ¹¹Believe Me that I am in the Father and the Father in Me, or else believe Me for the sake of the works themselves.

-John 14:9-11 | NKJV

God is Spirit and because we could not comprehend the glory of His unapproachable light, He covered Himself with flesh so He would be born and live among us. The fullness of the Godhead – Father, Son, and Holy Spirit was in His physical body.

Before Genesis 1:1, the Fatherhood characteristics of Jesus Christ were already establishment, who is the one and only heavenly Father we know.

40. Before Genesis 1:1, the Godhead was established for us to know that Jesus Christ is the Prince of Peace.

For unto us a Child is born, unto us a Son is given; and the government will be upon His shoulder. And His name will be called Wonderful, Counselor, Mighty God, Everlasting Father, PRINCE OF PEACE.

-Isaiah 9:6 | NKJV

Because Jesus Christ is the Prince of Peace, when He came into the world, there was no war recorded in history. Jesus Christ left all His glory, but He only came with His feet shod which is the gospel of peace which John the Baptist was not worthy to untie it.

It is He who, coming after me, is preferred before me, whose sandal strap I am not worthy to loose.

-John 1:27 | NKJV

When Simon Peter tried to wage war for Him by cutting someone's ear (Malchus), the Prince of Peace was there to bring peace.

It was Jesus Christ who brought the Gospel of peace for the restoration of the broken relationship between the souls of men and God and second between man and man. It was only His message that taught us that we should love our enemies.

Before Genesis 1:1, Jesus Christ knew there would be wars, kingdoms that would rise against the others, nations against nations in the world and sin that would bring war between man and God but it was only the Gospel He thought of bringing some day that would restore peace.

Chapter 11

THE RULERSHIP OF GOD THE FATHER IN THE FIRST ERA BEFORE GENESIS 1:1

No Authority

Let every soul be subject to the governing authorities. For there is NO AUTHORITY except from God, and the authorities that exist are appointed by God.

-Romans 13:1 | NKJV

The new universe needed one ruler. The reign was important to direct the things the Godhead had created. Humans, animals, plants, angels, and all other inanimate beings.

Let us get it straight in our world now. What do you think will happen when there are no pastors, parents, kings, presidents, principals, husbands etc in authority? The world will suffer leadership chaos and confusion.

The sheep will go wayward; children will be deviant; the people will find themselves in all kinds of social vices; the citizens will find themselves in all kinds of evil, the students will be uncontrollable; the wives will be less submissive and sin will be the order of the day.

The Godhead didn't want this to happen. They considered in afore-time that there must be a ruler amongst them to take the lead of the rulership over the universe they would create.

God The Father Ruled From Creation

Let the heavens rejoice, and let the earth be glad; and let them say among the nations, "THE LORD REIGNS."

-1 Chronicles 16:31 | NKJV

Since there were three Persons in the Godhead, all could not rule at the same time, they decided to rule in turns. They knew they would create images like themselves so they came into agreement that, if the three of them make themselves known to man, they would be confused. They then realized that there needed to be a set time of tenure.

As I am writing this, you will think that the Godhead cannot hold meetings to discuss certain issues. You know, God is not a robot who just does things without carefully analysing them. The physical things we do are sometimes what happens in the realms of the spirit.

God, holding meetings was clear during creation when man was about to be created. The subject 'us' in Genesis 1:26 depicts the three Persons of the Godhead who were thinking about what to do at that crucial time of creation.

Then God said, "Let US make man in Our image, according to Our likeness; let them have dominion over the fish of the sea, over the birds of the air, and over the cattle, over all the earth and over every creeping thing that creeps on the earth."

-Genesis 1:26 | NKJV

If humans can come together and discuss important issues and decide, then the Godhead is without excuse. I want you to realise that there were lots of things that went on behind the scenes before creation. If all things were written in the Bible, probably we wouldn't be able to contain them. I agree with John on this.

And there are also many other things that Jesus did, which if they were written one by one, I suppose that even the world itself could not contain the books that would be written. Amen.

-John 21:25 | NKJV

Rulership Of The Godhead On Earth Based On Era

Let all things be done decently and in order.

-1 Corinthians 14:40 | NKJV

God is a God of order and everything He does is in place. He is not an Author of confusion even before He created the universe. In that case, an agreement needed to be set in place by the Godhead to decide for sure some period of years they needed to put in place for their rulership.

The period they agreed upon were their own appointed era that they would make everything beautiful in its time.

He has made EVERYTHING BEAUTIFUL IN ITS TIME. Also He has put eternity in their hearts, except that no one can find out the work that God does from beginning to end.

-Ecclesiastes 3:11 | NKJV

God, The Father Takes The First Rulership Office

In the life of every being, there will be a first time. God has made us to understand many times He is the Alpha and also the first. This attribute makes us know Him well. Likewise, rulership or governance began with Him. The earth needed a President.

The cabinet in the persons of God the Son and the Spirit of God agreed for the 'Father' to be the first Head of the earth. We can see this governance in effect during the creation week. 'God said,' 'God saw,' 'God created,' and then 'Let us' were all signs of the Sovereignty of God the Father in action.

God The Father Appoints Man As His Prime Minister

Then God said, "Let Us make man in Our image, according to Our likeness; LET THEM HAVE DOMINION OVER THE FISH OF THE SEA, OVER THE BIRDS OF THE AIR, AND OVER THE CATTLE, OVER ALL THE EARTH AND OVER EVERY CREEPING THING THAT CREEPS ON THE EARTH."

-Genesis 1:26 | NKJV

Every ruler has His policies. One of the policies is to appoint people he can work with or people he can assign necessary duties to. Since God the Father became the President over man, He taught it wise to choose someone as His second in command to perform the duty of dominion over all the things that are not the images of God on earth for Him.

What Was The Other Godhead Doing?

The requirement of the other Godhead (Son and Spirit) had to sacrifice their display of power and infinite glory to support the reign of God the Father.

They also hid themselves in word (God the Son) and in truth (the Spirit of God) as helpers for God the Father during creation. They were not idle watching unconcerned about what was going on, but they also contributed their quota to the success of the reign of God the Father.

²The earth was without form, and void; and darkness was on the face of the deep. And the SPIRIT OF GOD was hovering over the face of the waters. ³Then GOD SAID, "Let there be light"; and there was light.

-Genesis 1:2-3 | NKJV

The other two Persons of God (Son and Spirit) became one in purpose, plan, and action. They supported God the Father to be first ruler, sitting on the throne and ruling in the affairs of the universe.

Symbolatry - The Condition Of Rulership For God The Father

Everything has a price one must pay for it. When I hear people say that the gifts they received was free, I reason that, that is not free because nothing is that free. Someone paid for the gift and there must be hidden charges attached to it which you will pay later on.

The condition of rulership was that, it was agreed between the Godhead that, God the Father should live in an unapproachable light and infinite glory so all creation might realise the infinite powers of deity.

The condition of rulership of God the Father was predetermined that He would rule in the form of shadow that would give glimpses of the nation of Christianity that would come later on.

That was why in the Old Testament, God had to reveal Himself in burning bushes, pillar of cloud, pillar of fire, and what have you. Since man could not see His face and live, He had to express Himself in symbols.

As an invisible God, His worshippers, or whom He was ruling over, needed something visible in the form of symbols to represent the invisibility of His existence of unapproachable presence.

Chapter 12

THE RULERSHIP OF GOD THE SON IN THE MID ERA BEFORE GENESIS 1:1

400 Silent Years

The period where God the Father was ending His tenure was the Silence years. That period there were no prophets, no judges, no king, and no priest. The world looked like a graveyard because the presence of God the Father was leaving for the next Godhead to take place.

This time took place from Malachi to Matthew. It took 400 years for God the Son to come to the earth for His term of rulership to begin. It was something that was predetermined (before Genesis 1:1).

Did The Father Create God The Son?

The Bible teaches that God the Son is a separate and distinct God who existed with the Father before everything was created. The Father did not create the Son; in fact, all the three Persons of God self existed from eternity. Carefully examine the words of John:

[1]That which was from the beginning, which we have heard, which we have seen with our eyes, which we have looked upon, and our hands have handled, concerning the Word of life - [2]the life was manifested, and we have seen, and bear witness, and declare to you that eternal life which was with the Father and was manifested to us —

-1 John 1:1-2 | NKJV

As eternal beings, the Father and the Son have no origin since the Son was with the Father before anything existed. John amplifies Jesus' eternal life with the following verses:

¹In the beginning was the Word, and the Word was with God, and the Word was God. ²He was in the beginning with God. ³All things were made through Him, and without Him nothing was made that was made. ¹⁴And the Word became flesh and dwelt among us, and we beheld His glory, the glory as of the only begotten of the Father, full of grace and truth.

-John 1:1-3, 14 | NKJV

There is no evidence in the Bible that the Father created the Son or that the Son is 'a lesser God' than the Father. The Bible reveals that from eternity, the Son has the same substance, power, glory, and authority as the Father and Holy Spirit! All three Persons of God are equal in every way.

We find the differences between them in their service. Now, please consider these two passages. The first passage shows that the Jews would not accept the idea that the Son was an equal to the Father and this made them very angry.

Therefore the Jews sought all the more to kill Him, because He not only broke the Sabbath, but also said that God was His Father, making Himself equal with God.

-John 5:18 | NKJV

The second passage affirms that the Son considered Himself equal with the Father. Paul wrote:

⁵Let this mind be in you which was also in Christ Jesus, ⁶who, being in the form of God, did not consider it robbery to be EQUAL WITH GOD, ⁷but

made Himself of no reputation, taking the form of a bondservant, and coming in the likeness of men.

-Philippians 2:5-7 | NKJV

Equality with the Father was not something that God the Son sought because He was 'in the very nature' of God.

The Decision To Make

Men were being ripped apart by sin. Every way of men was so mischievous that they needed someone to get them from the mess of sins and iniquities.

But the question is, how would this be achieved? How could it be done? Wasn't the blood of animals okay for God to totally cleanse the sins of humans once and for all? No! The blood of animals was only enough to cover the sins of men.

The board meeting between the three Persons of God was due, and many areas were being discussed. They are as follow:

1. The Specific Godhead To Come

After the rulership of God the Father, the onus now lied upon God the Son and the Spirit of God, who should take the baton to rule the earth. God, the Son was chosen to take the reins from the 'Father' after a successful meeting held by the Godhead.

2. Timing

The timing of the rulership was also discussed, and the decision was therefore taken. The period where the world is without hope; the time that the world earnestly expects a Messiah; the time that the prophesy concerning His coming delays and it looks like it will never happen. That was the time that the stage shall be set for the coming of God the Son as agreed between the Godhead.

3. The Mode Of Journey

One of the important discussions was how the Son will come from heaven to the earth to live amongst men. He opted to come very humbly.

You remember when Elijah was leaving earth? Chariots of fire which were pulled by fiery horses from heaven came to pick him up into the heavens. This dramatic departure could have been suggested by God the Son, or probably a more spectacular way that could have scared man the more.

When the Israelites saw the glory of God the Father on the mountains afar off, they were trembled, how much more the God the Son who shared similar glory with the Father stay with man? It could not be possible. That mode of journey would have made the journey a judgemental entry more than a salvation entry.

Agreement was reached for God the Son to become the 'voice of the Godhead' or 'Word of God' because He will be the mouthpiece or Speaker for the Godhead.

In other words, the Godhead would speak through one mouth. This explains why John saw a sharp sword coming from the mouth of God the Son in Revelation 19:15 and the name He had was THE WORD OF GOD.

[13]He was clothed with a robe dipped in blood, and His name is called THE WORD OF GOD. [14]And the armies in heaven, clothed in fine linen, white and clean, followed Him on white horses. [15]NOW OUT OF HIS MOUTH GOES A SHARP SWORD, that with it He should strike the nations.....

-Revelation 19:13-15 | NKJV

Now that God the Son would come through the Word, the carrier was now what needed to be decided. When the Godhead looked through the four living creatures, twenty-four elders, and all other angels, one angel was chosen among the lot.

The angel's name is called, Gabriel. He became the universal messenger angel of the Godhead. He was tasked to carry God the Son, who was the Word of God in His mouth.

4. Appearance For Operation

The next decision was to determine the appearance or form the God the Son should take for His rulership. A semblance of God or the semblance of man or semblance of an angel were all discussed upon.

Final decision was agreed that God the Son should take the semblance of a man (a bondservant), because taking the form of the people He was going to rule by saving them, was the best option.

5. Vessel To Carry Him

After it was made clear that He would be man, He needed to follow the trend of physicality. He needed to go through the natural way of conception. Since the Godhead was holy, they decided to choose an undefiled person in the name of a Virgin Mary to carry God the Son in her womb for nine months.

6. The Forerunner Determined

[2]As it is written in the Prophets: "Behold, I send MY MESSENGER BEFORE YOUR FACE, WHO WILL PREPARE YOUR WAY BEFORE YOU."

³"The voice of one crying in the wilderness: 'Prepare the way of the Lord; make His paths straight.'"

-Mark 1:2-3 | NKJV

The last thing on the list was the forerunner. What do I mean by a forerunner? A forerunner, in this case, is someone who will go before God the Son to indicate His approach or announce His coming.

You yourselves bear me witness, that I said, I AM NOT THE CHRIST,' BUT, I HAVE BEEN SENT BEFORE HIM.'

-John 3:28 | NKJV

The Prophets prophesied about his coming to prepare the way for God the Son and to make His paths straight. This forerunner had the Spirit of Elijah, who went before His ministration and His name was determined as John the Baptist.

He will also go before Him in the SPIRIT AND POWER OF ELIJAH, 'to turn the hearts of the fathers to the children,' and the disobedient to the wisdom of the just, to make ready a people prepared for the Lord."

-Luke 1:17 | NKJV

The Coming Of God The Son

We all know that God the Son was with the other Godhead in heaven before coming to earth to be born, but what actually happened before that? I am about to share with you systematically what actually happened.

The Stripping Offs

¹³**And in the midst of the seven lampstands One like the Son of Man, clothed with a garment down to the**

feet and girded about the chest with a golden band. ¹⁴His head and hair were white like wool, as white as snow, and His eyes like a flame of fire; ¹⁵His feet were like fine brass, as if refined in a furnace, and His voice as the sound of many waters; ¹⁶He had in His right hand seven stars, out of His mouth went a sharp two-edged sword, and His countenance was like the sun shining in its strength.

-Revelation 1:13-16 | NKJV

Before God the Son could come on earth, He didn't come with a grand or spectacular style with all His white horse, fiery eyes, head with crowns, blood cloth, armies, mouth with the tongue as a sword, rod of iron as His sign of rulership like some rulers use sceptres as a sign of authority and His thigh and vesture that had names written on them.

He stripped Himself off of all this kingdom, glory, power, dominion and all He had in Revelation 19:11-16. He then became ordinary, which is the form of a servant. He left all the things that made Him God in heaven and came with only peace.

⁶He had equal status with God but didn't think so much of himself that he had to cling to the advantages of that status no matter what. ⁷Not at all. When the time came, HE SET ASIDE THE PRIVILEGES OF DEITY and took on the status of a slave, became human!

-Philippians 2:6-7 | MSG

Acceptance To Be The Word

To be conceived in a woman's womb without sexual intercourse between a man and a woman, is not the natural order of conception. In that case, God the Son needed a certain process to enter the womb. One thing about the Word of God is that everything with Him is possible.

For with God nothing will be impossible.
-Luke 1:37 | NKJV

Even the entire universe and what we call 'nature' were all created by the Word that proceeded from the mouth of God. So, it was the Word of God only which was the beacon of hope to accomplish this mission.

Since God the Son is the Word of God, God the Father and the Spirit of God gave their prerogative rights to Him, that everything whether possible or impossible would be created through Him, by Him, and for Him.

[3]All things were made through Him, and without Him nothing was made that was made. [10]He was in the world, and the world was made through Him, and the world did not know Him.
-John 1:3, 10 | NKJV

The Metamorphosis

[7]But made Himself of no reputation, TAKING THE FORM OF A BONDSERVANT, and coming in the likeness of men. [8]AND BEING FOUND IN APPEARANCE AS A MAN, He humbled Himself and became obedient to the point of death, even the death of the cross.
-Philippians 2:7-8 | NKJV

The stripping off was not enough. He had to become a human to be born. The only way for God the Son to be a human was to be converted from Son of God into Son of man through the Word of God. The title that made us realise He had metamorphosed in that sense was for Him to be called 'Son of man.'

Gabriel Carries Him In His Mouth

As He became the word, the time was due for Him to enter into the carrier called Angel Gabriel. He then humbly entered the mouth of Gabriel in heaven (because He was the Word of God). Gabriel as a Messenger Archangel came to present Him to Mary, the virgin.

The Presentation

[30]Then the angel said to her, "Do not be afraid, Mary, for you have found favor with God. [31]And behold, you will conceive in your womb and bring forth a Son, and shall call His name Jesus. [32]He will be great, and will be called the Son of the Highest; and the Lord God will give Him the throne of His father David. [33]And He will reign over the house of Jacob forever, and of His kingdom there will be no end."

-Luke 1:30-33 | NKJV

Gabriel then presented God the Son to Mary the virgin through the Word of God (because the Word was not Gabriel's but God's). Here, you might think that, Gabriel was just trying to tell her who the baby was and how He was going to be born and all that, but spiritually, God the Son was in the mouth of the Archangel waiting for Mary to accept Him so He would abide in her womb.

[4]Abide in Me, and I in you. As the branch cannot bear fruit of itself, unless it abides in the vine, neither can you, unless you abide in Me.

[7]If you abide in Me, and My words abide in you, you will ask what you desire, and it shall be done for you.
-John 15:4, 7 | NKJV

The Supernatural Insemination

[34]Then Mary said to the angel, "How can this be, since I do not know a man?" [35]And the angel answered and said to her, "THE HOLY SPIRIT WILL COME UPON YOU, AND THE POWER OF THE HIGHEST WILL OVERSHADOW YOU; therefore, also, that Holy One who is to be born will be called the Son of God.
-Luke 1:34-35 | NKJV

Words are spirit (John 6:63) and as Mary accepted, believed, and confessed it, the Holy Spirit who took the universe from nowhere and filled it, formed God the Son through the word Mary believed, and He formed Him supernaturally in the womb of the virgin.

That was the only time the Spirit of God came on a mortal continuously for nine months, because what she was carrying was one of the Godhead in her. The Spirit of God protects everyone who has the Word of God abiding in him or her.

God The Son In Authority

For unto us a Child is born, unto us a Son is given; and the GOVERNMENT WILL BE UPON HIS SHOULDER. And His name will be called Wonderful, Counselor, Mighty God, Everlasting Father, PRINCE OF PEACE.
-Isaiah 9:6 | NKJV

The rulership of God the Son started when He was in the womb of Mary, the virgin. The first day of the divine conception was when He started ruling. John the Baptist in the womb of Elizabeth had to bow down to Him even in the womb of Mary as a sign of His authority. That caused the leaping of John the Baptist in his mother's womb.

And it happened, when Elizabeth heard the greeting of Mary, that the BABE LEAPED IN HER WOMB; and Elizabeth was filled with the Holy Spirit.

-Luke 1:41 | NKJV

The angel Gabriel proclaimed that He would be given the throne of His father David and what Isaiah prophesied that His government would be upon His shoulder will come to pass when the world will see Him carrying the cross on His shoulder on His way to Calvary.

The purpose of the cross (government) on His shoulder was a sign that His authority was His power over sin concerning those who are in the world. Through Him, men would regain authority over sin, which they lost in the Garden of Eden.

Before Genesis 1:1, the process of His first coming, the mission, and vision of the rulership or ministry of God the Son were predetermined.

[1]"The Spirit of the Lord God is upon Me, because the Lord has anointed Me to preach good tidings to the poor; He has sent Me to heal the brokenhearted, to proclaim liberty to the captives, and the opening of the prison to those who are bound; [2]To proclaim the acceptable year of the LORD, and the day of vengeance of our God; to comfort all who mourn, [3]to console those who mourn in Zion, to give them beauty for ashes, the oil of joy for mourning, the garment of praise for the spirit of heaviness; that

they may be called trees of righteousness, the planting of the Lord, that He may be glorified."

-Isaiah 61:1-3 | NKJV

Chapter 13

THE RULERSHIP OF THE SPIRIT OF GOD IN THE LAST ERA BEFORE GENESIS 1:1

The Outpouring Of One Branch Of The Spirit Of God

[28]"And it shall come to pass afterward that I WILL POUR OUT MY SPIRIT on all flesh; Your sons and your daughters shall prophesy, your old men shall dream dreams, your young men shall see visions. [29]And also on My menservants and on My maidservants I WILL POUR OUT MY SPIRIT IN THOSE DAYS.

-Joel 2:28-29 | NKJV

During the tenure of the office of God the Father, the Spirit of God was seen coming upon Kings and Prophets. What would have made Him come into them, was not there? That is the blood of Jesus Christ. He only comes *upon*, or be *with*, or be *on*, but not *in*. This was the only way He could fellowship with man in the Old Testament.

And Balaam raised his eyes, and saw Israel encamped according to their tribes; and the Spirit of God CAME UPON HIM.

-Numbers 21:2 | NKJV

The Spirit of truth, whom the world cannot receive, because it neither sees Him nor knows Him; but you know Him, for He DWELLS WITH YOU and WILL BE IN YOU.

-John 14:17 | NKJV

The Holy Spirit, one of the seven branches of the Spirit of God, was prophesied by the Prophet Joel, that He would come upon all flesh who are God's people.

Joel was not prophesying to the Gentiles here, but to Israel. Gentiles were not part of this inheritance till the death of Christ made us to be part, because He (God the Son) died for the world, not for Israel only.

He (Holy Spirit) was not working because He rested on the seventh day. Till the appointed time of Pentecost, He was seen resting in Genesis 2:2.

And on the seventh day God ended His work which He had done, and He rested on the seventh day from all His work which He had done.

-Genesis 2:2 | NKJV

The Secret Behind The Strength Of The Godhead

The reason God can never be defeated is that of the Spirit of God. God the Father is a spirit and so is God the Son. The secret I want to share with you concerning the Spirit of God is that the strength of the Godhead lies in the Spirit of God. Strength is not only physical but spiritual.

Samson is a typical example of someone who had the strength of God, which was spiritual. The seven dreadlocks on his head were the seven Spirits of God. He was the only mortal who could carry all the seven Spirits of God on his head, but He only utilised the Spirit of might as one of the seven Spirits of God. No wonder this spiritual strength made him have a powerful might to do extraordinary things physically.

The moment all the seven dreadlocks were shaved, the Spirit of God left him and he became an ordinary man bereft of strength.

¹⁹Then she lulled him to sleep on her knees, and called for a man and had him shave off the seven locks of his head. THEN SHE BEGAN TO TORMENT HIM, AND HIS STRENGTH LEFT HIM. ²⁰And she said, "The Philistines are upon you, Samson!" So he awoke from his sleep, and said, "I will go out as before, at other times, and shake myself free!" BUT HE DID NOT KNOW THAT THE LORD HAD DEPARTED FROM HIM.

-Judges 16:19-20 | NKJV

The Spirit Has Been With Us Since

.....And the Spirit of God was hovering over the face of the waters.

-Genesis 1:2 | NKJV

The Spirit of God has been with us since of creation as the One who moved over the face of the water in Genesis 1:2. From that time, He has been seeing coming upon the Prophets, Kings, and other people for carrying out the works of God.

Then Samuel took the horn of oil and anointed him in the midst of his brothers; and the SPIRIT OF THE LORD CAME UPON DAVID FROM THAT DAY FORWARD. So Samuel arose and went to Ramah.

-1 Samuel 16:13 | NKJV

But was He working officially like He was supposed to? No! It was until Jesus Christ left the scene that an agreement was reached between God the Father and God the Son to officially release Him to take over the final Presidency over the earth, specifically in the bodies of saints.

And I will pray the Father, and He will give you another Helper, that He may abide with you forever

-John 14:16 | NKJV

¹When the Day of Pentecost had fully come, they were all with one accord in one place. ²And suddenly there came a sound from heaven, as of a rushing mighty wind, and it filled the whole house where they were sitting. ³Then there appeared to them divided tongues, as of fire, and one sat upon each of them. ⁴AND THEY WERE ALL FILLED WITH THE HOLY SPIRIT and began to speak with other tongues, as the Spirit gave them utterance.

-Acts 2:1-4 NKJV

The Spirit Will Abide In Us Forever

And I will pray the Father, and He will give you another Helper, that HE MAY ABIDE WITH YOU FOREVER

-John 14:16 | NKJV

The walk with the Holy Spirit will not be a short term like that of the Father and the Son of the Godhead. The Holy Spirit will be in us forever until the second coming of Jesus Christ.

God the Father walked with the Israelites for a while. It was not even a daily abiding with the people, but a seasoned word that came to them. The Son also abided with the Israelites for 33 years and left, but the Holy Spirit is always abiding in us as He rules over the saints.

It is not everyone that the Holy Spirit is abiding in. It is only Christians that the Holy Spirit is living in forever. If a

Christian continues living in the sin he was saved from without repentance, the Holy Spirit has to leave the person and His restoration in you will be very difficult, even an impossibility.

⁴For it is impossible for those who were once enlightened, and have tasted the heavenly gift, and have become PARTAKERS OF THE HOLY SPIRIT, ⁵and have tasted the good word of God and the powers of the age to come, ⁶IF THEY FALL AWAY, TO RENEW THEM AGAIN TO REPENTANCE, since they crucify again for themselves the Son of God, and put Him to an open shame.

-Hebrews 6:4-6 | NKJV

Chapter 14

THE ESTABLISHMENT OF ONE FAMILY OF THE GODHEAD BEFORE GENESIS 1:1

For there are three that bear witness in heaven: the Father, the Word, and the Holy Spirit; and these three are one.

-1 John 5:7 | NKJV

The Family Of The Godhead

How can three distinct people stay together for eternity, created time and have since lived to this point with no misunderstanding, conflict, war or any other situation emerging out?

What is the secret did they have that believers can also learn from? As we are created in their image, why can't we also live peaceably with other humans in our families, workplaces, schools, churches, societies and countries?

If it is possible, as much as depends on you, live peaceably with all men.

-Romans 12:18 | NKJV

Love is the defining secret behind the relationship between God the Father, God the Son, and the Spirit of God. For example, when Jesus came to earth, He came to do the will of the Father who sent Him (John 6:38) out of love.

Jesus Christ surrendered Himself to the will of the Father. That is what the Holy Spirit is also doing now. He has surrendered His will to God the Son in doing His will out of love.

The love they have for one another produced a universe without conflict or competition. The Godhead knew that even though they are three (three Persons in the Godhead), their created beings would need one God they will serve.

Why is Family More Important to God?

1. Family is important to God, because the Godhead is a family of three people.

And because you are sons, GOD has sent forth the SPIRIT of His SON into your hearts, crying out, "Abba, FATHER!"

-Galatians 4:6 | NKJV

Family is a social unit living together; a primary social group of parents and children; collection of things sharing a common attribute, and an association of people who share common beliefs or activities.

Trinity or the Godhead is a family of three Persons (God the Father, Son, and Spirit). It is not just abstract entities, but real Personalities who exist.

God is one family because the Godhead is a unit of three Persons who are living together. God is one family because the Godhead is a group of a Parent (God the Father) and children (God the Son).

God is one family because the Godhead is a collection of three Persons who share a common attribute of being. God is One family because the Godhead is the association of three Persons who share common beliefs or activities of holiness, righteousness, and sanctification.

2. Family is important to God, because as a woman, submitting to your husband is submitting to God.

Wives, SUBMIT to your own husbands, AS TO THE LORD.

-Ephesians 5:22 | NKJV

A family is a unit of a husband, wife, and children. Family is very important to God, because it makes the will of God is done in the lives of women who marry. Marriage will lead many people to hell, but marriage will also help others saved.

Marriage is not a curse, and marriage should not be seen as a bad thing. It is God who instituted marriage in the first place, and He did it for the purpose of salvation.

One will of God about families is that wives should submit to their husbands. Doing so, they fulfil their submission to God. If you truly submit yourself to Jesus Christ, then it will reflect in your marriage.

3. Family is important to God, because as a man, loving your wife is loving God.

Husbands, love your wives, just as Christ also loved the church and gave Himself for her,

-Ephesians 5:25 | NKJV

If Jesus Christ is the head of the church and your wife is also the church of Jesus Christ, then loving the wife who is a church, is loving the head of the church who is Jesus Christ. So those Pastors who have divorced their wives without the reason of sexual immorality don't love God.

You can profess you love God by your lips, but your heart is far from Him if you don't obey His commandments (John 14:15). Husbands who love their wives, also love God, and such a family is ruled by God.

4. Family is important to God, because it is the will of God for the leadership of the husband to be established over the wife.

> **But I want you to know that the head of every man is Christ, THE HEAD OF WOMAN IS MAN, and the head of Christ is God.**
>
> **-1 Corinthians 11:3 | NKJV**

Family is very important to God because God wants to establish leadership right from the foundation. He wants authority to be established so we will know how to lead and how to submit ourselves to our leaders.

Marriage is the institution for achieving such a purpose of leadership. It is because we don't lead well and we can't submit well under authorities that is why there are disorderliness, conflicts, wars in our world today.

No matter how rich you are as a wife, how literate you are, how beautiful you are and all that, you have to realise the truth that your husband is your head. Give him the necessary respect as you do for your Pastors.

> **.....let the wife see that she respects her husband.**
>
> **-Ephesians 5:33 | NKJV**

5. Family is important to God, because God wants His leadership over the husband to be established.

> **But I want you to know that the HEAD OF EVERY MAN IS CHRIST, the head of woman is man, and the head of Christ is God.**
>
> **-1 Corinthians 11:3 | NKJV**

They are mainly broken homes just because many husbands are ungodly. If you really fear God, you will not divorce your wife for no reason. If you truly fear God, you will not marry more than one and have concubines as your attachments.

If Jesus Christ reigns on a husband, he will make sure he also leads the rest of the family in the Lord. He will train his children in the right way they should go. The best inheritance he will leave for the family is the Lord.

6. Family is important to God, because male children are God's heritage and female children are His reward.

Behold, children are a HERITAGE from the Lord, the fruit of the womb is a REWARD.
-Psalms 127:3 | NKJV

Family is important to God because the children that parents procreate are the heritage and rewards of God. If you know that children are the heritage and rewards of God, you will never abort your babies.

How can value your house, money, lands, businesses, etc more than a soul? There is nothing in this world that can be used as an exchange for a soul. Because children are heritage and rewards of God, He knows how He will take care of them.

You can't even take care of yourself, why do you think you can't take care of a baby and for that reason you are aborting? Everyone depends on God because it is Him who provides everything for us.

You wouldn't say you will do family planning just to control the birth of babies if you know that children are God's heritage and rewards. Imagine if Mary aborted Jesus Christ, what would have been the fate and destiny of the world?

7. Family is important to God, because obedience of parents by children, is obedience to Him.

CHILDREN, OBEY YOUR PARENTS IN ALL THINGS, for this is WELL PLEASING TO THE LORD.

-Colossians 3:20 | NKJV

Pleasing God is one will of God about families. What is the essence of having young ones in the church if they are not pleasing God? Instead of children obeying their parents in the Lord, they rather obey their friends in the world.

8. Family is important to God, because after God, the nuclear family comes next.

⁴One who RULES HIS OWN HOUSE WELL, having his children in submission with all reverence ⁵(FOR IF A MAN DOES NOT KNOW HOW TO RULE HIS OWN HOUSE, HOW WILL HE TAKE CARE OF THE CHURCH OF GOD?);

-1 Timothy 3:4-5 | NKJV

After God, the nuclear family comes next. I know you were thinking about the church. The church is very important, but the nuclear family is most important. Christianity is not demonstrated in the church, but in your home.

You can fake holiness in church, but you can't fake holiness in your home. What is so serious is that, before you can become a Minister of God, you must first take care of your nuclear family. If you take care of your household well, then it is a sign that you can take care of the church of God.

Many wives honour, respect, and submit to their Pastors more than their husbands. That is wrong. Your husband is first the head in your home before the Pastor in the church. That hierarchy of leadership should be respected.

9. Family is important to God, because after the nuclear family, the spiritual family comes next.

For whoever does the will of My Father in heaven is My brother and sister and mother.

-Matthew 12:50 | NKJV

Jesus Christ has purchased us with His blood from the various tribes, languages, nations, and peoples into the spiritual family and nation called Christianity, which is the kingdom of heaven.

As you are responsible in your household, don't neglect the church. If there is any person we have to invest much in, it is the people in the church who do the will of God. There are many people who don't do the will of God, yet they want to be helped financially.

A brother, a sister, mother, and father in the Lord is someone who does the will of God. That person is the church and not the church building. Even though you have to cater for your physical family but don't neglect those who are of the spiritual household.

But if anyone does not provide for his own, and especially for those of his household, he has denied the faith and is worse than an unbeliever.

-1 Timothy 5:8 | NKJV

After Jesus Christ started His ministry, He gave more attention to His spiritual family than His physical family. In the presence of His physical family, He declared those He was ministering to as His real family.

10. Family is important to God, because if we see everyone as our neighbour or family, it will be easier for us to love those who love us and love those who hate us.

And the second, like it, is this: You shall love your neighbor as yourself.' There is no other commandment greater than these."

-Mark 12:31 | NKJV

The reason many of us cannot love others like ourselves is that we don't see them as our family or neighbours. A neighbour in Christ is not someone who lives or is located near you, but someone of the same kind as you.

Every human being has his kind who is also a human bring. If we see every human being as us, we will not hurt them like we don't want to hurt ourselves. We will see ourselves in them and them also in us.

The secret behind the love between the Godhead is that the Son sees Himself in the Father and the Father likewise; the Son sees Himself in the Spirit and the Spirit likewise; the Father sees Himself in the Spirit and the Spirit likewise.

Love Is What Makes The Family Of God One

[7]Beloved, let us love one another, for love is from God, and whoever loves has been born of God and knows God. [16]So we have come to know and to believe the love that God has for us. God is love, and whoever abides in love abides in God, and God abides in him.

-1 John 4:7, 16 | NKJV

Because love makes two fleshes one (Genesis 2:24), love also made the three Persons of God, One. God, the Son and the Father are one because of love. The Holy Spirit and the Son are one because of love. The Spirit and the Father are also one with the Father because of love.

I and My Father are one."

-John 10:30 | NKJV

Now the Lord is the Spirit; and where the Spirit of the Lord is, there is liberty.

-2 Corinthians 3:17 | NKJV

They also knew that God's family would need one God (Jesus Christ) to live among created beings as a created being showing everyone about the manifestation of God the Father who is in an unapproachable light on the throne.

Finally, the Godhead knew that humanity would need one God (the Holy Spirit) to live within them so they could have instant and simultaneous communication with the Father whom they can't see His face and live.

This arrangement puts God above, besides, and within every living being within the universe! They hoped that God would be present in every place or heart in the universe (this explains why the Holy Spirit is omnipresent now, but the Father and Jesus were not).

To accomplish their goals, three equal Gods surrendered prerogatives to each other and this amazing union is called love. Therefore, the Bible says that God is love. This declaration means that the Godhead dynamically shows and defines every aspect of love 'in proper time.'

It is amazing that three infinitely powerful and glorious three Persons of God are constrained by nothing. It is because of love they have to live and work together for the happiness and welfare of their family (Godhead).

Anywhere there is love, there is joy, peace, long-suffering, kindness, goodness, faithfulness, gentleness, and self-control.

²²But the fruit of the Spirit is love, JOY, PEACE, LONGSUFFERING, KINDNESS, GOODNESS, FAITHFULNESS, ²³GENTLENESS, SELF-CONTROL.....

-Galatians 5:22-23 | NKJV

God the Son is the perfect reflection of the Father. The Father is also the perfect reflection of God the Son and the Holy Spirit. In other words, the Father would have died for us if that had been necessary. In fact, it was Him who was in the Son reconciling us to Himself.

That is, that GOD WAS IN CHRIST RECONCILING THE WORLD TO HIMSELF, not imputing their trespasses to them, and has committed to us the word of reconciliation.

-2 Corinthians 5:19 | NKJV

Moreover, the Holy Spirit is a perfect reflection of the Son and the Father, and He is willing to remain invisible for eternity so the glorious Father will be glorified as the supreme Ruler of the Universe.

The mutual surrender between equals is mentioned by Jesus Christ several times.

¹⁰Do you not believe that I am in the Father, and the Father in Me? The words that I speak to you I do not speak on My own authority; but the Father who dwells in Me does the works. ¹¹Believe Me that I am in the Father and the Father in Me, or else believe Me for the sake of the works themselves.

-John 14:10-11 | NKJV

Privacy?

We all want to be excused one way or the other. We often like being in our comfort zones and out of reach from our families, friends, and people we are not even acquainted with. As humans, we don't like everything about us to be exposed? Probably not. Privacy is why we have so many secrets.

The Godhead knew man would want to be excused to do his or her own thing, but they knew their will for their lives must be established (Matthew 6:10). I often hear people say, *'God has given everyone his or her will to misbehave and for that reason, everyone can do what he or she likes.'*

Those whom God's will is not done in their lives are sinners and not those who fear Him. If you are doing your will for your children, do you include a stranger who is locked up in a prison for so many years? No way! You include someone in your will because they person honour and obey you.

You don't include people in your will who are unworthy of your trust even if the person is your biological son or daughter. Likewise, God's will is not done for those who are not His children. Before He can do so, unless they are first saved from their sins and do as He wills.

"Not everyone who says to Me, Lord, Lord,' shall enter the kingdom of heaven, BUT HE WHO DOES THE WILL OF MY FATHER IN HEAVEN.
-Matthew 7:21 | NKJV

After salvation, God will then lead you in all your Godliness, ministry, and everything that pertains to your life.

It is the best thing for God to lead you in everything you do. Let God lead you and what you have to do is to follow

Him. Many people are leading the way, and God is rather following them.

When they hit the dead end, they turn back to God for help. The Godhead is always ready to engage in our affairs. Are we indeed ready to give them the opportunity so they can have their family in us?

Chapter 15

THE CALLED GENERATIONS BEFORE GENESIS 1:1

Who has performed and done it, CALLING THE GENERATIONS FROM THE BEGINNING? 'I, the Lord, am the first; and with the last I am He.' "

-Isaiah 41:4 | NKJV

The Book Of Records

God told Prophet Jeremiah that He knew him before he was born. If you know someone, you also know the person's name. Before someone can be born, his name is already recorded in the Book of Records.

Before Genesis 1:1, God was preparing this book that would contain all the names of angels and all the names of human beings that would come in this world. For those who are not having their names recorded in the Book of Records can never be born.

It is medically proven that the semen of a man contains a million of sperms and at least one of these millions of sperms can fertilise with one ovum of the woman he is having the sexual intercourse with.

It is believed that the healthy sperm that gets there first is the sperm that can fertilise and become a baby. So, in this view, the millions of sperms are taking part in some kind of race. The one who has his name written in the Book of God's Book of Records, is the one will win the race to the mother's ovum for fertilisation.

Someone will ask, what if the woman has a miscarriage or when the baby is aborted from being born at all? The day the sperm and the ovum fertilise is the day the child is born and not when the child comes out of the womb.

So, if you have miscarriage or have an abortion thinking it is just a clot of blood, God knows that soul. God knew Jeremiah not when he was fully developed in his mother's womb but before he was even formed, thus in the zygote stage.

"BEFORE I FORMED YOU IN THE WOMB I KNEW YOU; BEFORE YOU WERE BORN I sanctified you; I ordained you a prophet to the nations."

-Jeremiah 1:5 | NKJV

All the generations that would come even before the world began, God had written already all their names in the Book of Records. So, God knows everyone who is dead, is still living or will be born in the future.

The Vision of Daniel

A fiery stream issued and came forth from before Him. A thousand thousands ministered to Him; ten thousand times ten thousand stood before Him. The court was seated, and the BOOKS WERE OPENED.

-Daniel 7:10 | NKJV

Daniel seeing books opened in heaven after the Ancient of Days sat on the throne gives us glimpses of the Book of Records, Book of Remembrance, and the Book of life.

Many of us know much about the Book of life and not the Book of Records. Before the Ancient of Days can judge, the book that contains the names of those who have ever existed, must be opened and checked for evidence.

All generations that have ever existed, have all their names in the Book of Records as part of the books Daniel saw were opened in the court of the Ancient of Days.

The Revelation of John

And I saw the dead, small and great, standing before God, and BOOKS WERE OPENED. And another book was opened, which is the Book of Life. And the dead were judged according to their works, by the things which were written in the books.

-Revelation 20:12 | NKJV

Another evidence of the Book of Records in the Bible is the revelation Apostle John had. He saw that books were opened during judgement, as Daniel also saw, but this judgement was called 'The Judgement of The Great White Throne.'

Before God can judge, He cannot forego the Book of Records. Everyone that had been called forth as a generation has his or her name written in the Book of Records.

Every mortal who once lived has his or her name written in the Book of Records, but it is those who made it to the end in the Lord are those whose name can be written in the Book of life.

1. Before Genesis 1:1, the Godhead knew that all generations would not cross the 7000 years mark of the end of the world.

But the heavens and the earth which are now preserved by the same word, are reserved for fire until the day of judgment and perdition of ungodly men.

-2 Peter 3:6 | NKJV

Though it looks like the universe was made to stay forever or because Adam sinned, that was why the plan changed, but the Lord made the world not to exist all the time. The universe had an expiry date determined by God.

The Lord took six days in the sight of man but 6000 years in His sight to create the universe and used one day in the sight of man but 1000 years in His sight to rest, making 7000 years. This gives us the hint that the expiry date God gave to the universe to exist, was 7000 years at most.

We are not here in this expiry world to live all the time as a generation who have been called forth. The generations that needed to be called forth to fill the universe would not cross the 7000 years mark of the universe before the world began as predetermined by the Godhead.

2. Before Genesis 1:1, the Godhead knew the generation of the first 2000 years era He would call forth.

[34].....the son of Abraham, the son of Terah, the son of Nahor, [35]the son of Serug, the son of Reu, the son of Peleg, the son of Eber, the son of Shelah, [36]the son of Cainan, the son of Arphaxad, the son of Shem, the son of Noah, the son of Lamech, [37]the son of Methuselah, the son of Enoch, the son of Jared, the son of Mahalalel, the son of Cainan, [38]the son of Enosh, the son of Seth, the son of Adam.....

-Luke 3:34-38 | NKJV

The generations can be separated into three main eras according to the expiry date of the universe. The first generation in the first 2000 years starts from the time of Adam to the time of Abraham.

All the names of these mortals were recorded to come in that space of time. God programmed the coming of the generations that needed to come at that time.

The most important event in the lives of the generation that lived at the time of the first 2000 years was the flood that happened during the time of Noah.

3. Before Genesis 1:1, the Godhead knew the generation of the second 2000 years era He would call forth.

[23]Now Jesus Himself began His ministry at about thirty years of age, being (as was supposed) the son of Joseph, the son of Heli, [24]the son of Matthat, the son of Levi, the son of Melchi, the son of Janna, the son of Joseph, [25]the son of Mattathiah, the son of Amos, the son of Nahum, the son of Esli, the son of Naggai, [26]the son of Maath, the son of Mattathiah, the son of Semei, the son of Joseph, the son of Judah, [27]the son of Joannas, the son of Rhesa, the son of Zerubbabel, the son of Shealtiel, the son of Neri, [28]the son of Melchi, the son of Addi, the son of Cosam, the son of Elmodam, the son of Er, [29]the son of Jose, the son of Eliezer, the son of Jorim, the son of Matthat, the son of Levi, [30]the son of Simeon, the son of Judah, the son of Joseph, the son of Jonan, the son of Eliakim, [31]the son of Melea, the son of Menan, the son of Mattathah, the son of Nathan, the son of David, [32]the son of Jesse, the son of Obed, the son of Boaz, the son of Salmon, the son of Nahshon, [33]the son of Amminadab, the son of Ram, the son of Hezron, the son of Perez, the son of Judah, [34]the son of Jacob, the son of Isaac, the son of Abraham,

-Luke 3:23-34 | NKJV

The second generation of another 2000 years era, making it 4000 years, began from Abraham to the time of Jesus Christ. Before Genesis 1:1, God knew this second batch of generation that He would call forth and positioned them according to His will.

One of the major events concerning the end of the world during this time, is the destruction of Sodom and Gomorrah with fire and brimstone as an event of the end of the world that would soon come to pass.

4. Before Genesis 1:1, the Godhead knew the last generation of the third 2000 years era He would call forth.

The last generation is from the time of Jesus Christ till the last baby who will be formed in the womb of his or her mother before the second coming of Jesus Christ.

Before Genesis 1:1, God knew everyone who would be born after the time of His first coming because He had all their names in His Book of Records.

This teaching is very important in the sense that we are not here, not because we wanted to come, but because there is a God who predestined all these things before the world even began. We ought to humble ourselves and respect everyone because we don't know the identity of the people we are dealing with.

Throughout the generations, God came as a man and lived among us, yet many people didn't know His identity. We are all here to fulfil the will of the Godhead who knew us before we were even born.

5. Before Genesis 1:1, the Godhead knew the third and fourth generation whom they would visit their iniquity upon them.

You shall not bow down to them nor serve them. For I, the Lord your God, am a jealous God, VISITING THE INIQUITY OF THE FATHERS UPON THE CHILDREN TO THE THIRD AND FOURTH GENERATIONS OF THOSE WHO HATE ME,

-Exodus 20:5 | NKJV

If you are a believer, one prayer you must pray to be delivered from, is for God to deliver you from the impact of the sins your family has committed.

There are many struggles believers are going through just because of the sins some people committed some time ago that they have no idea about in the family and the nation as a whole. Sin is what brings curses that affect generations.

If we can fully function in our Christian walks, we have to overcome the generational curses that we find ourselves in. We have to identify those curses so we can know how we can pray about it and live our lives well in the Lord so we will not be overcome by those curses.

Everyone who sins is cursed, and that affects the person's children too, because the Godhead visits the iniquity of the person, not only him, but upon the third and fourth generations of that cursed person.

Before Genesis 1:1, God already knew the generation that would rebel against Him. God knew that Pharaoh would not let the Israelites go, unless compelled by a mighty hand, yet He sent Moses to him.

God knew very well that the people were obstinate, their necks were like iron sinews and their brows bronze, yet He sent Isaiah to them. God is not taken by surprise concerning the inactions of the generation to come because He is aware of the deviant generations He called before the world even began.

6. Before Genesis 1:1, the Godhead knew the thousands who would love Him, keep His commandments, and whom His mercy would be shown.

But showing mercy to thousands, to those who love Me and keep My commandments.

-Exodus 20:6 | NKJV

Before you can love God unless you first have the grace of God. You can't love God with your own will. There are so many people in your family who are ungodly, but have you asked yourself why you are godly?

If you love God and keep His commandments, you automatically get the mercy of God. The mercy of God is not for sinners who are not ready to repent, but for those who are. It is the Lord's mercy we are not consumed by sin.

Through the Lord's mercies we are not consumed, because His compassions fail not.

-Lamentations 3:22 | NKJV

The Godhead knew those who would love Him and keep His commandments because it was Him who chose such generation before the world began.

Just as HE CHOSE US IN HIM BEFORE THE FOUNDATION OF THE WORLD, that we should be holy and without blame before Him in love,

-Ephesians 1:4 | NKJV

7. Before Genesis 1:1, the Godhead established their covenant with the 1000 generations who would remember it forever.

Remember His covenant forever, the word which He commanded, for a thousand generations,

-1 Chronicles 16:15 | NKJV

To have a covenant with someone is through the sacrifice of blood. At first the Lord kept His covenant with His people through the sacrifice of the blood of animals, which was temporary because it couldn't remove the sins of the people but only covered them.

But the covenant the Godhead established forever with the thousands of generations was the blood shed by God Himself. This is the covenant God has with the souls of saints forever leading to eternal life through the seal of the Holy Spirit.

Chapter 16

THE LOVE OF GOD THE FATHER BEFORE GENESIS 1:1

The grace of the Lord Jesus Christ, and the LOVE OF GOD, and the communion of the Holy Spirit be with you all. Amen.

-2 Corinthians 13:14 | NKJV

The love of God has since been with man, even from the beginning. Without the love of God, the Godhead would not have created the heavens, and the earth in the first place. This is because the Godhead was okay living in their secret place.

Unselfishness, which indicates love, is what the Godhead had, that was why they created the universe in the first place. It was the love of God that made God create angels, some who would be the elect and those who would fall.

God knew that some angels He was creating would be His enemies or rebel against Him, yet He created them. God knew that Adam and Eve and some of their descendants would sin against Him some time to come, but He created them.

It was because of love that made God create them, even though He had such a foreknowledge about the fate of the creations He was creating.

Sometimes when children go wayward, many mothers think it was a bad idea not to have had aborted them if they knew what their deviant children would become in the future. If many mothers would have been God, sinners wouldn't have been created at all.

God Loves Both His Lovers And His Enemies

⁴⁵.....He makes His sun rise on the evil and on the good, and sends rain on the just and on the unjust.....³⁵For He is kind to the unthankful and evil.
-Matthew 5:45; Luke 6:35 | NKJV

When men say we love someone, it is mainly because of who you are, what you have done and what you can do for him or her. The love of men is usually opportunistic, but the love of God is without partiality.

God doesn't love those who love Him only but those who hate Him. He gives both His lovers and His enemies breath of life. He wakes both His lovers and His enemies from sleep. He provides them with food, water, clothing, shelter and what have you with their wants.

God provides His enemies beautiful wives to marry and beautiful children as well. God doesn't say you are my enemy, so when I am raining or shining, I will be biased towards you. NEVER!

The Greater Love

For God so loved the world that He gave His only begotten Son, that whoever believes in Him should not perish but have everlasting life.
-John 3:16 | NKJV

The greater love that the Father of the Godhead had for His enemies was when He sacrificed His one and only Son to come and die for us. Before Genesis 1:1, He knew how He would show His greater love by sacrificing His Son.

As in happened in the Old Testament when Isaac the only legitimate son of Abraham whom he had sacrificed him so it also re-echoed in the New Testament when God also sacrificed His one and only Son.

Who will ever think of giving his one and only beautiful daughter to his fierce enemy's son to marry? Even if you don't like your daughter because of her deviant behaviour, you will never give her hand in marriage to your enemy.

Jesus Christ was not a deviant Son in the bosom of the Father, but a beloved Son who obeyed the commandments of His Father and abided in His love. You can't be in someone's bosom if you don't love the person.

No one has seen God at any time. THE ONLY BEGOTTEN SON, WHO IS IN THE BOSOM OF THE FATHER, He has declared Him.

-John 1:18 | NKJV

If you keep My commandments, you will abide in My love, JUST AS I HAVE KEPT MY FATHER'S COMMANDMENTS AND ABIDE IN HIS LOVE.

-John 15:10 | NKJV

The Father loved the Son so much because of His submission to Him. The love that existed between God the Father and God the Son was such of a kind, and that love gave rise to the Father glorifying the Son even before the world was made.

And now, O Father, glorify Me together with Yourself, with the glory which I had with You before the world was.

-John 17:1 | NKJV

Before God the Father showed His love through the sacrifice of His own Son, He predetermined the timing of His coming from heaven to earth, womb to earth, His ministry, His death, resurrection and ascension.

1. Before Genesis 1:1, God the Father knew His children who because of His love, would love their enemies.

But LOVE YOUR ENEMIES, do good, and lend, hoping for nothing in return; and your reward will be great, and YOU WILL BE SONS OF THE MOST HIGH. For He is kind to the unthankful and evil.

-Luke 6:35 | NKJV

One of the difficult things on earth is to love your enemies. Without the love of God, you can never love those who have offended you and have proved to you they are reluctant to change.

Before we can be sons of God, we have to love our enemies. Loving our enemies is making peace with those who have offended us. To love your enemies is to be a peacemaker.

Blessed are the peacemakers, for they shall be called sons of God.

-Matthew 5:9 | NKJV

As long as we are in the body, mortals will offend us. Even if God the Son with all the sanctified, righteous, and holy life He was living, many people still offended Him and His words also offended others.

[61]When Jesus knew in Himself that His disciples complained about this, He said to them, "DOES THIS OFFEND YOU? [66]From that time many of His disciples went back and walked with Him no more.

-John 6:61, 66 | NKJV

It is because of offences that turn a loved one into an enemy and if you want to be a child of God, then you have to reconcile your enemies to yourself and love them as you love those who love you. As God loves us, so should we love others unconditionally.

For this is the message that you heard from the beginning, that we should love one another,

-1 John 3:11 | NKJV

2. Before Genesis 1:1, God the Father knew His children who because of His love, would bless those who would curse them.

.....bless those who curse you.....

-Matthew 5:44 | NKJV

Serving God means: been subject to or been prone to verbal abuses. Jesus Christ was not having any evil spirit living in Him, yet He was verbally abused that He was having the spirit of Beelzebub that was why He could cast out devils.

Now when the Pharisees heard it they said, "This fellow does not cast out demons except by Beelzebub, the ruler of the demons."

-Matthew 12:24 | NKJV

Before the Sanhedrin, He was verbally accused of many things He had not done, yet; He didn't respond to any. That is what the Father wants us to be. He doesn't want us to respond to bad things people say about us, which is not true.

[62]And the high priest arose and said to Him, "DO YOU ANSWER NOTHING? What is it these men testify against You?" [63]BUT JESUS KEPT SILENT.....

-Matthew 26:62-63 | NKJV

You will be accused or cursed, but you may not have done that. You don't have to prove yourself right by swearing, instead, tell them what the truth of the matter is. Let your yes be yes and not be no.

³⁴But I say to you, do not swear at all: neither by heaven, for it is God's throne; ³⁵nor by the earth, for it is His footstool; nor by Jerusalem, for it is the city of the great King. ³⁶Nor shall you swear by your head, because you cannot make one hair white or black. ³⁷But let your 'Yes' be 'Yes,' and your 'No,' 'No.' For whatever is more than these is from the evil one.

-Matthew 5:34-37 | NKJV

Instead of wishing something bad happens to your enemies, wish them well. Bless those who curse you. Always let your words be seasoned with salt, even in the presence of your enemies so you will know how to tame your tongue from uttering filthy words.

Let your speech always be with grace, seasoned with salt, that you may know how you ought to answer each one.

-Colossians 4:6 | NKJV

Before Genesis 1:1, God knew His children who would bless those who would curse them. He already knew that those who cannot be His children would not bless those who would curse them.

3. Before Genesis 1:1, God the Father knew His children who, because of His love, would pray for those who would persecute them.

.....pray for those who spitefully use you and persecute you,

-Mathew 5:44 | NKJV

Another proof that we are God's children is the proof of intercession for our enemies and not judgemental prayers against them. If you are a Christian, the kind of prayer you pray, tells it all.

We have two principal enemies: physical enemies (human beings), and spiritual enemies (fallen angels). We have to resist the spiritual enemies with prayer and the Word of God, but for physical enemies; we have to pray for them.

Today, there are many believers who pray and send fire to burn their physical enemies. No mortal can sin or offend you without the influence of an evil spirit. The sin or evil the person offended you with, he or she was ignorant of it, because it was the work of evil spirit(s) behind that action.

"Yet now, brethren, I know that YOU DID IT IN IGNORANCE, as did also your rulers.

-Acts 3:17 | NKJV

If we know this, we will never be at loggerheads with anyone. Because of the evil spirit behind the action of the person, we have to pray for them so God can deliver them from that evil spirit so they can be at liberty to do what is right as Jesus Christ did in Luke 23:34.

Then Jesus said, "FATHER, FORGIVE THEM, FOR THEY DO NOT KNOW WHAT THEY DO....."

-Luke 23:34 | NKJV

Before Genesis 1:1, God already knew His children who would not only pray for themselves or those they love, but those who are their enemies.

4. Before Genesis 1:1, God the Father knew His children who, because of His love, would do good to those who would hate them.

…..do good to those who hate you…..

-Matthew 5:44 | NKJV

Because of the love of God, He does good to those who hate Him. He rains and shines for those who hate Him as an evidence of His goodness.

It is not those who are good to us alone that we need to be good towards. There are people who give gifts to those who have already given them too. They have never given to those who have never given to them before.

When Jesus Christ was teaching the people, He told them the will of the Father concerning goodness. Many Jews were good to their neighbours only, and not those who had nothing to offer them.

5. Before Genesis 1:1, God the Father knew His children who, because of His love, would lend and expect nothing in return.

…..lend, hoping for nothing in return…..

-Luke 6:35 | NKJV

Love is also about giving or lending without the expectation of payback. When you love someone, you want to give the person your time, money, attention, strength, and everything you have to care for the person to earn his or her love.

When we give all these things, what we expect in return is not any material need but the person's love. Normally for those who give to people not because of love, they do so, expecting what they did in return.

When they give you money, they expect money in return. When they give you their time by coming to your wedding, they expect you to give them your time by coming to their wedding, otherwise all hell will break loose.

All hell didn't break loose for God when, after giving His own Son for us, got nothing in return even though He was not expecting it. See what men did to His own Son for the love He showed to us, yet He never gave up on us.

Under normal circumstance, anytime we lend, we always expect the person to pay back, but sometimes we know that the person cannot pay it back and we must cancel that debt.

If we love God and man, we should not be stingy in giving. If it is offering or tithing or any almsgiving, it is like we are lending to God, but we should give with the expectation of blessings from God.

He who has pity on the poor lends to the Lord, and He will pay back what he has given.

-Proverbs 19:17 | NKJV

It is a blessing to lend than to borrow. Let that be the motivation why you must give.

FOR THE LORD YOUR GOD WILL BLESS YOU just as He promised you; YOU SHALL LEND TO MANY NATIONS, BUT YOU SHALL NOT BORROW; you shall reign over many nations, but they shall not reign over you.

-Deuteronomy 15:6 | NKJV

Instead of expecting something from God, we must remember and be grateful to God for what He has done for us on the cross. It should be an honour or a privilege to give to God always.

Before Genesis 1:1, God was aware of His children who could lend to Him and their fellow human beings without expecting anything in return as a means of sacrifice.

6. Before Genesis 1:1, God the Father knew His children who, because of His love, would not expect nothing in return for the good things they do for their enemies.

.....do good.....hoping for nothing in return.....

-Luke 6:35 | NKJV

It is one thing to *lend* expecting nothing and one thing to do *good* expecting nothing in return, even though they are all about giving.

Lending is like giving out a loan which you expect the person to pay back but yet, God still wants us to expect no payment otherwise it would ruin the relationship we have with the person if he cannot pay on time.

I had to cancel the debt two people owed me because I realised they couldn't pay. As I was constantly expecting them to pay, my heart was not at peace at all until I cancelled their debts.

Doing good on the other hand expecting nothing in return, too, is different. With lending, the person asks you to give him what he needs, but with doing good it is not like that. It is you who is giving what the person may need or want, and that is where the problem lies.

Because goodness is doing things which are pleasing, valuable or useful in the lives of others lies in your power, many people do not do it right. Like Cain, they give what is not the best but what is bad and that is not what God wants.

Anyone who does good at its best knows it, and many of those people expect others to return that favour but when they do goodness which is below par, they don't expect such thing to be returned in their favour.

IF YOU DO WELL, WILL YOU NOT BE ACCEPTED? And if you do not do well, sin lies at the door. And its desire is for you, but you should rule over it."

-Genesis 4:7 | NKJV

If we want to do good, we have to learn from Abel, who gave his best shot in his offering to God. We have to think of Jesus Christ who, because of His love for His enemies, gave His best shot by dying on the cross to save us from our sins.

ABEL ALSO BROUGHT OF THE FIRSTBORN OF HIS FLOCK AND OF THEIR FAT. And the Lord respected Abel and his offering,

-Genesis 4:4 | NKJV

Before Genesis 1:1, God was aware of His children who, because of His love, would be good to their enemies expecting nothing in return.

7. Before Genesis 1:1, God the Father knew His children who would love Him with all their hearts.

And you shall love the Lord your God with all your heart.....

-Mark 12:30 | NKJV

The heart is the focus point for belief. If we love God, we should believe Him always. Having faith in God pleases Him so much. Abraham had faith in God, and it was counted onto him as righteousness. Without faith in Jesus Christ, righteousness can't be imputed into us.

And the Scripture was fulfilled which says, "ABRAHAM BELIEVED GOD, AND IT WAS ACCOUNTED TO HIM FOR RIGHTEOUSNESS." And he was called the friend of God.

-James 2:23 | NKJV

If we say we love God, we should believe Him in good times and in bad times. Many believers doubt God when they go through serial persecutions but they still claim they love God.

When there is money, the love for God is different and when there is no money, the love for God is also different. We shouldn't let anything separate us from the love we have for God in our hearts.

Nor height nor depth, nor any other created thing, shall be able to separate us from the love of God which is in Christ Jesus our Lord.

-Romans 8:39 | NKJV

Many believers say they love their partners with all their heart, and that is blasphemy. You can't love someone with all your heart if you claim you are a believer. God is the One you have to love with all your heart and not a man or a woman.

Many people get disappointed for loving someone. Many people are broken-hearted beyond mending when they love people with all their heart, which should not have been the case. When you love people with all your heart, which it rightfully belongs to God, you will face the adverse consequences.

We serve God because of love and not because of New Jerusalem, and that demands the totality of our hearts. Don't give all your heart to a girl or a boy you are madly in lust with.

Before Genesis 1:1, God knew His children who would not love Him with part of their hearts but with all their hearts.

Blessed are those who keep His testimonies, who seek Him with the whole heart!

-Psalms 119:2 | NKJV

8. Before Genesis 1:1, God the Father knew His children who would love Him with all their souls.

And you shall love the Lord your God…..with all your soul…..

-Mark 12:30 | NKJV

It is very dangerous to love God with your body and not with your soul. There are people who love God physically and not spiritually. The body will die and will rot, but the soul lives on eternally. That is why the soul has to love God.

Many people love God on the outside, but deep inside them (thus in their souls), they don't. That is what God was saying, that these people draw near me with their mouths and honour me with their lips but they have removed their heart far from me (Isaiah 29:13). Many people don't just love God with their hearts, but their souls.

As there are physical and spiritual realms, there are two versions of you: the body and the soul. If you truly love God in your body, it should translate into your soul as a real proof of your love for God.

If you love God with your soul, you will see it in your dreams. To love God is to do His commandments. So, if you dream and you always do things that are not right in your dream, then it is a wake-up call.

Don't just brush off the events of your soul when you dream. They are glimpses of what your soul loves and hates.

If you love God, you will see it and if you don't, you will know. If you are not yet born again, your soul cannot love God as he ought to.

If the body loves God and the soul does not, you cannot have eternal life. Before you can love God with all your soul, unless you first accept Jesus Christ into your soul so you can be changed from the inside out.

Before Genesis 1:1, God knew His children who would love Him with their souls and not just their bodies. We should not just love God outwardly, but inwardly. If we truly love God, we have to be changed inwardly for the better.

9. Before Genesis 1:1, God the Father knew His children who would love Him with all their minds.

And you shall love the Lord your God…..with all your mind…..

-Mark 12:30 | NKJV

When Joshua succeeded Moses, He was entreated by God to meditate on the Word of God day and night.

This Book of the Law shall not depart from your mouth, but you shall meditate in it day and night, that you may observe to do according to all that is written in it. For then you will make your way prosperous, and then you will have good success.

-Joshua 1:8 | NKJV

To love God is to meditate on the Word of God all the time. God is the same as His Word (John 1:1) and if we think about His Word daily, we are loving Him in our minds.

As a man thinks, so is he. If we love God and we always attempt to think about sin, then our love for God is not right.

To love God is to do what is right, and if we love God with all our minds, then it will reflect in our behaviours.

The mind is one of the powerful gifts God has given to humanity but that same gift, when not taken proper care of, can land us into big trouble, preventing us from working out our own salvation with fear and trembling.

Before Genesis 1:1, God was aware of His children who will not just love Him with their hearts and souls but with all their minds as well.

10. Before Genesis 1:1, God the Father knew His children who would love Him with all their strength.

And you shall love the Lord your God.....with all your strength.' This is the first commandment.

-Mark 12:30 | NKJV

King Solomon was advised by his mother not to give his strength to women. As a youth, you will be tempted to waste your strength on youthful lusts that will not get you anywhere of which when you get old, you will regret it later on.

Do not give your strength to women, nor your ways to that which destroys kings.

-Proverbs 31:3 | NKJV

If you are to ask many grown-ups, they will testify that they had wasted their years when they were youth - wasting their strength on alcoholism, sex, night club partying, smoking, and what have you.

We are to remember God by loving Him as youth when we have all the strength at our disposal and not when we grow old or when we become sick. The strength to carry out the works of our salvation and the work of God will not be there anymore.

¹Remember now your Creator in the days of your youth, before the difficult days come, and the years draw near when you say, "I have no pleasure in them": ⁶Remember your Creator before the silver cord is loosed, or the golden bowl is broken, or the pitcher shattered at the fountain, or the wheel broken at the well.

-Ecclesiastes 12:1, 6 | NKJV

You have the strength to lift your wife who is 100kg during sex but you can't lift up church speakers when there is crusade which matters most. You see that you love your wife with all your strength and not God.

Many people have the strength to do secular work, but they don't have that same strength to do ministerial work. They will never sleep in their workplaces but they will always sleep in church and when you advise them, they will tell you their action is justifiable because they are tired.

The love of God requires vitality, and that is exactly what God has placed in us before Genesis 1:1 so we can love Him. Everything we need to have so we can love God, He has already given to us.

And from the days of John the Baptist until now the kingdom of heaven suffers VIOLENCE, and the violent TAKE IT BY FORCE.

-Matthew 11:12 | NKJV

11. Before Genesis 1:1, God the Father knew His children who would love others as themselves.

And the second, like it, is this: You shall love your neighbor as yourself.' There is no other commandment greater than these."

-Mark 12:31 | NKJV

To love others like ourselves, it is not that easier to do if you don't have the love of God in you. Judgement will be based on the relationship we have with our fellow human beings.

If we love others as ourselves, we will never offend them. The simplest way of becoming righteous is through love. When we say we love someone, we try as much as possible to please them and not to grieve them.

We try to please them by doing what they want so we will not hurt their feelings and inasmuch as that, lose them in the process. It is high time we loved our fellow human beings as we claim we love God.

If someone says, "I love God," and hates his brother, he is a liar; for he who does not love his brother whom he has seen, how can he love God whom he has not seen?

-1 John 4:20 | NKJV

Before Genesis 1:1, the Father of the Godhead knew His children who would love others as a proof that their love for God is not just a hoax.

By this we know that we love the children of God, when we love God and keep His commandments.

-1 John 5:2 | NKJV

Chapter 17

THE GRACE OF GOD THE SON BEFORE GENESIS 1:1

THE GRACE OF THE LORD JESUS CHRIST, and the love of God, and the communion of the Holy Spirit be with you all. Amen.

-2 Corinthians 13:14 | NKJV

The grace of Jesus Christ is what makes the difference. If angels had the grace of God the Son, they wouldn't have been jealous of human beings.

For the law was given through Moses, but GRACE and truth came through JESUS CHRIST.

-John 1:17 | NKJV

They are jealous because when man sinned against God; He sent God the Son to die for them, but when their fellow angels rebelled against Him, God the Son wasn't sent to save them.

For God did not send His Son into the world to condemn the world, but that the world through Him might be saved.

-John 3:17 | NKJV

The reason angels don't spare disobedient children when they are sent to destroy them, is because of the grace of the Son of God their fellow fallen angels have been deprived of.

God has told no angel he is his son before and He will not do that because they don't have the grace that should be made available for receiving that power to become a child of God. Without the grace of God, no one can become a child of God.

For to which of the angels did He ever say: "You are My Son, today I have begotten You"? And again: "I will be to Him a Father, and He shall be to Me a Son"?

-Hebrews 1:5 | NKJV

Noah – The First Person To Find Grace

But Noah found grace in the eyes of the Lord.

-Genesis 6:8 | NKJV

Noah, being the first human Evangelist (eighth Evangelist) wouldn't have been chosen by God to carry out his ministry of evangelism without grace. Before you begin ministry, make sure you have first found grace in the eyes of God. Don't just begin ministry just because you feel you are called.

The question we have to ask ourselves is that what was Noah doing that made him find grace in the eyes of God? In the following verse, after Noah found grace in the sight of God, the Bible tells us why it was Noah alone who found grace in his entire generation.

This is the genealogy of Noah. NOAH WAS A JUST MAN, PERFECT IN HIS GENERATIONS. NOAH WALKED WITH GOD.

-Genesis 6:9 | NKJV

In Genesis 6:9, first, Noah was a just man. Second, Noah was perfect in his generations. Third, Noah walked with God. Many people think they can have grace doing nothing for it, and anyone can have it just as they feel they want it.

You can see from the world Noah found himself in, that it was corrupt before God and was also filled with violence. The wickedness of man was great, and every intent of their hearts was only evil continually.

Then the Lord saw that the wickedness of man was great in the earth, and that every intent of the thoughts of his heart was only evil continually.

-Genesis 6:5 | NKJV

You can't live in sin claiming you are a child of God and still expect grace to give you eternal life. Even if God wants to save a sinner with His grace, He knows that after that grace is shown, the sinner will not continue living in his sin.

¹What shall we say then? Shall we continue in sin that grace may abound? ²Certainly not! How shall we who died to sin live any longer in it? ³Or do you not know that as many of us as were baptized into Christ Jesus were baptized into His death? ⁴Therefore we were buried with Him through baptism into death, that just as Christ was raised from the dead by the glory of the Father, even so we also should walk in newness of life. ⁵For if we have been united together in the likeness of His death, certainly we also shall be in the likeness of His resurrection, ⁶knowing this, that our old man was crucified with Him, that the body of sin might be done away with, that we should no longer be slaves of sin. ⁷For he who has died has been freed from sin.

-Romans 6:1-7 | NKJV

Grace is not there for us to continue living in sin. Grace was not shown to Noah for him to continue living in his sin. Grace is not just a privilege or a license to give people the liberation to sin, but a responsibility for one to stop sinning.

Whoever has been born of God does not sin, for His seed remains in him; and he cannot sin, because he has been born of God.

-1 John 3:9 | NKJV

Jesus Christ – The Epitome Of Grace

And the Word became flesh and dwelt among us, and we beheld His glory, the glory as of the only begotten of the Father, FULL OF GRACE and truth.

-John 1:14 | NKJV

From the Old Testament, many people found grace in the eyes of God, but they only saw the shadow of grace and not the reality of who grace was. It was in the New Testament that grace became flesh and lived among us for us to behold His glory.

And the Word became flesh and dwelt among us, and we beheld His glory, the glory as of the only begotten of the Father, full of grace and truth.

-John 1:14 | NKJV

Grace is not just a thing that we can find, but grace is a Person and His name is Jesus Christ. If we say we have grace and still sin, then we don't have the grace we are claiming we are having.

Without the grace of Jesus Christ, you can't have the love of God. Christianity is about steps and if you miss one, you cannot grow spiritually. You first need to have the grace of Jesus Christ before you can fully love God and man.

Grace Before Genesis 1:1

The Book Of Life

All who dwell on the earth will worship him, whose names have not been written in the Book of Life of the Lamb slain FROM THE FOUNDATION OF THE WORLD.

-Revelation 13:8 | NKJV

The greatest grace is for your name to be written in God the Son's Book of life. Because God the Son knew before Genesis 1:1 that some day He would die and save men from their sins, He first wrote the names of all those whom He would save.

You can claim you are a child of God because you go to church because of the grace of God but your name may not be in the Book of Life. You can claim you are a Christian just because you pray or fast everyday. If your name is not yet written in the Lamb's book of life, then you have not yet had the grace of God the Son.

When people wake up from bed and you ask them what they are doing, the response you normally get is that, '*by the grace of God, I am fine.*' It seems everyone knows that it takes the grace of a higher power to keep them alive.

Everyone knows that there is a grace that keeps them alive physically, but they don't seek after the grace that will keep their souls alive, eternally.

The grace of God the Son is all about salvation for those who would have faith in Him to receive it. Because God the Son knew the people whom His grace of salvation would benefit, their names were written before Genesis 1:1.

[27]My sheep hear My voice, and I know them, and they follow Me. [28]And I give them eternal life, and they shall never perish; neither shall anyone snatch them out of My hand.

-John 10:27-28 | NKJV

What Is It Like To Have The Grace Of God the Son?

To have the grace of Jesus Christ, there are many things that show and things you can also benefit from the grace of God the Son.

It is not everyone who can have the grace of God the Son. When we give birth to children, the one who respects, submits him or herself to us, and obey us, are the ones who will be highly favoured in our sight.

To show someone grace, there must be something that must first be done. Before God the Son came to save us with His grace, He knew His sheep were yearning for His salvation. The one who is poor is the one who needs help and not the one who is prosperous.

When Jesus heard it, He said to them, "Those who are well have no need of a physician, but those who are sick. I did not come to call the righteous, but sinners, to repentance."

-Mark 2:17 | NKJV

The 5 Benefits of the Grace of God the Son

1. When you have the grace of God the Son, you inadvertently get favour in the eyes of people.

[8]And now for a little while GRACE HAS BEEN SHOWN FROM THE LORD OUR GOD, to leave us a remnant to escape, and to give us a peg in His holy place, that our God may enlighten our eyes and give us a measure of revival in our bondage. [9]For we were slaves. YET OUR GOD DID NOT FORSAKE US IN OUR BONDAGE; BUT HE EXTENDED MERCY TO US IN THE SIGHT OF THE KINGS OF

PERSIA, to revive us, to repair the house of our God, to rebuild its ruins, and to give us a wall in Judah and Jerusalem.

-Ezra 9:8-9 | NKJV

Getting grace in the eyes of God will make you have favour in the eyes of other people. Many believers yearn for certain favours which cannot be attained, but instead of them doing the things that will make them have grace in the sight of God, they think they can garnish it on their own.

As you can't force people to genuinely love you so you can't force yourself on someone so you can have his favour. It is something that has to come naturally and not something that must be coerced.

For you to have favour in the eyes of someone, you need a higher power. People have certain favours because of the great people they associate themselves with. Having relationships with great people will definitely make others have the impression that you are also a great person.

If we have relationship with God as the greatest person, His greatness will rub off on us and this will also affect our relationship with other people.

If we have unmerited divine kindness, assistance, clemency or special favour from God, others too will have it for us because His grace does not only have influence on us but has influence on those who are around us.

2. When you have the grace of God the Son, there is a peaceful relationship between your soul and God.

[19]For it pleased the Father that in Him all the fullness should dwell, [20]and by Him to reconcile all things to Himself, by Him, whether things on earth or things

in heaven, having made peace through the blood of His cross.

²¹And you, who once were alienated and enemies in your mind by wicked works, yet now He has reconciled ²²in the body of His flesh through death, to present you holy, and blameless, and above reproach in His sight—

-Colossians 1:19-22 | NKJV

The greatest relationship is to have a cordial relationship between your soul and God. The grace Christians have that sinners don't have, is the peaceful relationship between their souls and God.

In fact, there are worldly people when you have relationship with them, you will even ruin your relationship with God.

Blessed is the man who walks not in the counsel of the ungodly, nor stands in the path of sinners, nor sits in the seat of the scornful;

-Psalms 1:1 | NKJV

We can't have a peaceful relationship with God based on our own works, and that is why we need grace. We need that divine mercy which is part of grace to connect us to God. Without it, doing good cannot make us righteous before God.

It is because of a peaceful relationship between our souls and God, that was why He sent His Son to come and die for us so we can be reconciled to Him and our sins could be forgiven. Without grace, we will be enemies of God always.

3. When you have the grace of God the Son, it gives you salvation.

For the GRACE OF GOD that BRINGS SALVATION has appeared to all men,

-Titus 2:11 | NKJV

To have the grace of God is to be saved permanently from sin. Without the acceptance of the grace of God the Son on the cross for you and I, we couldn't pass any other way to get on level terms with God.

Jesus said to him, "I am the way, the truth, and the life. No one comes to the Father except through Me.

-John 14:6 | NKJV

If we know what sin can do to our souls, we will never reject the love of God and His offer of grace to save us. Sin is a killer of our souls, and if we can ever be healed, we need the blood of God the Son to cleanse us.

Furthermore, there is a place reserved for those who will not accept the grace of God the Son in their lives – an eternal place which is so horrible beyond every possible imagination called the lake of fire.

Even though it is not advisable to accept the grace of God the Son based on the fear of the lake of fire, but it is a wise decision if you do so. It is better to fear God than to live well and reject His grace.

4. When you have the grace of God the Son, you attract divine visitation.

³As he journeyed he came near Damascus, and suddenly a light shone around him from heaven. ⁴Then he fell to the ground, and heard a voice saying to him, "Saul, Saul, why are you persecuting Me?" ⁵And he said, "Who are You, Lord?" Then the Lord said, "I am Jesus, whom you are persecuting. It is

hard for you to kick against the goads." ⁶So he, trembling and astonished, said, "Lord, what do You want me to do?" Then the Lord said to him, "Arise and go into the city, and you will be told what you must do."

-Acts 9:3-6 | NKJV

When the Lord visits you, His principal mission is to save you. When angels sinned, God the Son didn't visit them to die for them, but when men sinned, God the Son came to die for them. If it was not of grace, what else?

For God to come down and mingle in the affairs of men was at its best when He came as man. When we check through the Bible, concerning those whom God visited, it didn't come without grace. It is not everyone that the Lord visits.

Before the Persecuting Paul became the Preaching Paul, he first had divine visitation on his way to Damascus and that was the turning point in his life towards salvation.

³As he journeyed he came near Damascus, and suddenly a light shone around him from heaven. ⁴Then he fell to the ground, and heard a voice saying to him, "Saul, Saul, why are you persecuting Me?" ⁵And he said, "Who are You, Lord?" Then the Lord said, "I am Jesus, whom you are persecuting. It is hard for you to kick against the goads." ⁶So he, trembling and astonished, said, "Lord, what do You want me to do?" Then the Lord said to him, "Arise and go into the city, and you will be told what you must do."

-Acts 9:3-6 | NKJV

If you don't have the grace of God the Son, there cannot be any divine visitation to cause you to repent. Even though you will be preached to, without the grace of God the Son, you will never repent.

There are so many people out there who have heard the Word of God so many times, but they don't have salvation. There are many believers in churches now, and yet they are still sinning.

A lot of those who were once in other religions have seen God the Son in their dreams before they were converted, while many believers have been serving God without knowing the God they serve. Without grace, God cannot visit you.

5. When you have the grace of God the Son, whatever you want, you will get it without struggle.

Let us therefore come boldly to the THRONE OF GRACE, that we may obtain MERCY AND FIND GRACE TO HELP IN TIME OF NEED.
-Hebrews 4:16 | NKJV

It was because of the grace Noah found in the eyes of God, that was why God spared the pair of animals He kept in the ark. You will bear with me that the rest of the animals who were not kept in the ark were all destroyed.

God saw that if He destroyed all animals, Noah and his family would have nothing to eat after the flood. When grace locates you, you won't struggle to get what to eat, what to drink, where to lay your head down, and what you need or want won't be any problem.

"Therefore I say to you, do not worry about your life, what you will eat or what you will drink; nor about your body, what you will put on. Is not life more than food and the body more than clothing?
-Matthew 6:25 | NKJV

Our heavenly Father is the owner of every riches and wealth. If we serve Him well, His grace will influence our wealth both physically and spiritually.

Chapter 18

THE FELLOWSHIP OF THE SPIRIT OF GOD BEFORE GENESIS 1:1

The grace of the Lord Jesus Christ, and the love of God, and the COMMUNION OF THE HOLY SPIRIT be with you all. Amen.

-2 Corinthians 13:14 | NKJV

The reason God created the universe and most especially man, was all because He wanted to have a fellowship with a being of His kind – His image and likeness He could also call a Son.

[26]Then God said, "Let Us make man in Our image, according to Our likeness; let them have dominion over the fish of the sea, over the birds of the air, and over the cattle, over all the earth and over every creeping thing that creeps on the earth." [8]And they heard the sound of the Lord God walking in the garden in the cool of the day.....

-Genesis 1:26; 3:8 | NKJV

If you study the pattern of the things God created, He created them in kinds. Even in plants, there are kinds. Plants normally have a seed that has the potency of reproducing according to their kind.

[11]Then God said, "Let the earth bring forth grass, the herb that yields seed, and the fruit tree that yields fruit according to its kind, whose seed is in itself, on the earth"; and it was so.

¹²And the earth brought forth grass, the herb that yields seed according to its kind, and the tree that yields fruit, whose seed is in itself according to its kind. And God saw that it was good.

-Genesis 1:11-12 | NKJV

A parent plant fellowships with its offsprings because it is of its kind. What comes out of you is seen as your own. A plant offspring shares a common characteristic which it inherited from its parent that differs it from the rest of other plants.

When it comes to a higher organism like an animal, there is a special thing called 'blood' that connects animals of their kind. It is that powerful link that serves as a covenant between animals of their kind.

And God made the beast of the earth according to its kind, cattle according to its kind, and everything that creeps on the earth according to its kind. And God saw that it was good.

-Genesis 1:25 | NKJV

Without blood, there is no covenant and when there is no covenant, there is no fellowship.

For this is My blood of the new covenant, which is shed for many for the remission of sins.

-Matthew 26:28 | NKJV

For a fellowship to be binding forever, there must be a covenant in blood. The reason many believers have not yet tasted the Lord and seen His goodness is because they don't have any fellowship with Him.

As animals have fellowship with their own, through blood, it is only through the blood of God the Son that can connect us to God the Father and Him to us. This is what brings about the covenant between our souls and His Spirit. This is the only means that we can really worship God in truth and in Spirit.

The Holy Spirit can never have fellowship with you until the blood of God the Son has been smeared on the doorpost of your soul crossing you from death to life. It is only then that the Holy Spirit can befriend your soul.

David-Jonathan Friendship – A Glimpse Of The Fellowship Of The Holy Spirit And Our Souls

Fellowship Is A Spiritual Knitting

Now when he had finished speaking to Saul, the soul of Jonathan was knit to the soul of David, and Jonathan loved him as his own soul.

-1 Samuel 18:1 | NKJV

The friendship of Jonathan and David in the Old Testament was a glimpse of the fellowship of the Holy Spirit and the saints in the New Testament.

When we dive into the friendship of Jonathan and David, it was more of a spiritual fellowship than a physical one. Before they could become friends, the soul of Jonathan has to knit to the soul of David.

To knit is to tie or link firmly or closely; to cause to grow together; to become drawn together. This is what normally happens when you have sex with someone.

Your souls are knitted together through sexual intercourse as you exchange fluid. Sex is more spiritual than physical, and that is why God cautions us against sexual immorality. It takes deliverance by an anointed Minister to break such soul ties.

His soul was strongly attracted to Dinah the daughter of Jacob, and he loved the young woman and spoke kindly to the young woman.

-Genesis 34:3 | NKJV

Past relationships can haunt you even when you get married, and this is one reason many people marry and commit adultery with their former boyfriends or girlfriends. Some even divorce in the process.

Indeed, evil communication corrupts good manners because the kind of fellowship you have with someone has a rightful or wrongful consequence on your spirituality. That is why your soul has to get a holy spiritual friend who will have a positive influence on his spiritual life.

Fellowship Is A Covenant

THEN JONATHAN AND DAVID MADE A COVENANT, because he loved him as his own soul.

-1 Samuel 18:3 | NKJV

After the soul of Jonathan and David was knitted together, both of them made a covenant. That is what also happens when the Spirit of God fellowships with us. The covenant is done through the blood of God the Son.

A covenant without blood has no spirit backing it. Because many families have made covenant with blood, they are dead and gone, yet the spirits that backed those covenants through the blood they shed, are still alive to keep such fellowship with the rest of the family.

When covenants are made, there is an agreement on both parties to carry out certain tasks. If we have fellowship with the Spirit of God, we have to live a life without sin to keep the covenant, and the Spirit of God can continue staying in us.

Fellowship Has Benefits

And Jonathan took off the robe that was on him and gave it to David, with his armor, even to his sword and his bow and his belt.

-1 Samuel 18:4 | NKJV

Every relationship has its benefits, so it is when your soul has fellowship with the Spirit of God. Before David became friends with Jonathan, the Prince, he didn't get any privilege to get near the Prince's royal clothing.

Before David became friends with the Prince, he was not getting access to the Prince's defensive weapon (armour) and he was not privileged to be entrusted in his hands, the offensive weapon (sword) of the Prince too.

We will not get what the Spirit of God has to offer us until we start fellowship with Him. The Spirit of God is wealthy both spiritually and physically, and He is ever ready to bless us materially and immaterially if we fellowship with Him till he end of our lives on earth and beyond.

1. Before Genesis 1:1, the fellowship of the Spirit of God was established to enhance the fellowship of the saints.

That which we have seen and heard we declare to you, that you also may HAVE FELLOWSHIP WITH US; and TRULY OUR FELLOWSHIP IS WITH THE FATHER AND WITH HIS SON JESUS CHRIST.

-1 John 1:3 | NKJV

When your soul becomes friends with the Holy Spirit, He leads you to have fellowship with your kind. If the Holy Spirit leads you to fellowship with sinners, then it is for the purpose of evangelism and soul winning.

When the Holy Spirit communes with your soul, there will always be a burning desire in you to attend church meetings. It was before the 120 disciples started fellowshipping together in the upper room that made the Holy Spirit descend into them.

The fruits of the Holy Spirit are love and peace and He will never lead you to distant yourself from people even when they offend you. He will always give you the reason and to the urge of togetherness to be with other saints.

Because the Holy Spirit in you and the Holy Spirit in me are the same, they will surely connect or knit together. When the spirit of lust is in you and you meet another person who also has the same spirit, you will be sexually attracted to each other.

If there is no unity in the church, then it means the congregation has different spirits. If anyone has an excuse to miss church always, then it means the fellowship of the Holy Spirit leading to assembling of saints, is not working in that person.

NOT FORSAKING THE ASSEMBLING OF OURSELVES TOGETHER, as is the manner of some, but exhorting one another, and so much the more as you see the Day approaching.

-Hebrews 10:25 | NKJV

Before Genesis 1:1, the Spirit of the Godhead saw that without assembling of the saints, His presence cannot be in their midst.

For where two or three are gathered together in My name, I am there in the midst of them."

-Matthew 18:20 | NKJV

It was important for saints to meet for them to be exhorted, so none would be swayed away from the faith as the end of the world approaches.

2. Before Genesis 1:1, the fellowship of the Spirit of God was established, so it would be impossible for saints to sin.

IF WE SAY THAT WE HAVE FELLOWSHIP WITH HIM, AND WALK IN DARKNESS, we lie and do not practice the truth.

-1 John 1:6 | NKJV

Adam and Eve never sinned until Satan influenced them to do so. There cannot be any evil or any sin that can ever be committed without the influence of evil spirits and you cannot practise holiness for the rest of your life without the fellowship of the Spirit of God.

Whoever has been born of God does not sin, for His seed remains in him; and he cannot sin, because he has been born of God.

-1 John 3:9 | NKJV

As His name is holy, so He is. He will always influence you to stay away from all sins so you can be holy (thus sins of omission). He will also help you to do the commandments of the Word of God so you can stay holy (thus sins of commission).

Sins of omission are the sins we do that God has told us to do away or refrain from so we can be holy and sins of commission are the things we have to do that if we don't do them, will make us unholy or imperfect before Him.

There are many things that are sin, but when you don't have the fellowship of the Spirit of God, you may never know. That is why it is needful to have the Spirit of God in us, otherwise we can't love God by keeping His commandments.

Today, many people think they have the fellowship of the Spirit of God just because they can speak in tongues, but the greatest manifestation is holiness. Without holiness, no man can see the Lord and not speaking in tongues.

Pursue peace with all people, and holiness, without which no one will see the Lord:

-Hebrews 12:14 | NKJV

3. Before Genesis 1:1, the fellowship of the Spirit of God was established to give rise to various ministrations of the saints.

Imploring us with much urgency that we would receive the gift and the FELLOWSHIP OF THE MINISTERING TO THE SAINTS.

-2 Corinthians 8:4 | NKJV

When you have the fellowship of the Holy Spirit, He will give you a ministry. When we talk about ministry, many people think that it is only about the fivefold ministry. There are many ministries beyond the fivefold ministry that God the Son gives.

Someone can have the fellowship with the Holy Spirit, but he may not be an Apostle, Prophet, Evangelist, Pastor or Teacher, yet we are all ministers of the Gospel and that is the good work we all have to do.

5For your FELLOWSHIP IN THE GOSPEL from the first day until now, 6being confident of this very thing, that He who has begun a GOOD WORK in you will complete it until the day of Jesus Christ;

-Philippians 1:5-6 | NKJV

Ministries of the Spirit of God include the ministry of miracles, healing ministry, helping ministry, administrative ministry, and ministry of linguistics.

.....after that miracles, then gifts of healings, helps, administrations, varieties of tongues.
-1 Corinthians 12:28 | NKJV

The helping ministry can be those who have dedicated themselves to give financially to support the work of God. The helping ministry can be church workers such as ushers, singers, prayer towers, voluntary artisans who help build the house of God and maintain it without payment, and among others.

Without the fellowship of the Spirit of God, you cannot have the power to perform miracles, healings, administrative roles, and speaking of varieties of languages. When you have the fellowship of the Spirit of God, you can never be idle in the house of God. You will certainly get something to do.

4. Before Genesis 1:1, the fellowship of the Spirit of God was established to give rise to the mysteries of the kingdom of God.

And to make all see what is the FELLOWSHIP OF THE MYSTERY, WHICH FROM THE BEGINNING OF THE AGES HAS BEEN HIDDEN IN GOD who created all things through Jesus Christ;
-Ephesians 3:9 | NKJV

There are many things hidden in God, and it takes the fellowship of the Holy Spirit to unravel such mysteries. When the disciples became friends with God the Son, the things He kept from the crowd, He revealed to them.

He answered and said to them, "Because it has been given to you to know the mysteries of the kingdom of heaven, but to them it has not been given.

-Matthew 13:11 | NKJV

When you get closer to someone, the person will tell you many secrets about him or her that those who are distant from him or her can never know. *The more you get closer to someone, the more you know the person.*

Because Abraham fellowshipped with God when He became three men, He couldn't keep the secret about the destruction of Sodom and Gomorrah from him. He had to tell him what He was about to do.

And the Lord said, "Shall I hide from Abraham what I am doing,

-Genesis 18:17 | NKJV

There are many mysteries about the Word of God, and we need the Spirit of God as the Teacher to impart the true understanding behind the Scriptures to us. Without Him, we will interpret the Scriptures based on our carnal conscience.

But the Helper, the Holy Spirit, whom the Father will send in My name, He will teach you all things, and bring to your remembrance all things that I said to you.

-John 14:26 | NKJV

5. Before Genesis 1:1, the fellowship of the Spirit of God was established to bring unity in the body of Jesus Christ.

Therefore if there is any consolation in Christ, if any comfort of love, if any FELLOWSHIP OF THE SPIRIT, if any affection and mercy, fulfill my joy by being LIKE-MINDED, HAVING THE SAME

LOVE, BEING OF ONE ACCORD, OF ONE MIND.

-Philippians 2:2 | NKJV

The varieties of ministry must connect us together and not disconnect us. Today when someone becomes an Apostle in a church, the next move is to start his own church so it is for some Prophets, Evangelists, Pastors, and Teachers. But this should not have been the case.

As there are many members of the body, but they come together as one, so must we be. Even though there are different ministrations in the church, we have to be one. The church needs all ministrations so she will profit and not lack in any.

Also, no matter our nationality, the language we speak, the family, tribe, or clan we come from, whether we are slaves or masters or whether we are males or females, we are one people in the Lord and there should not be any ground of discrimination.

Today, many churches prevent women from carrying out ministry. After the death of God the Son, the veil of the temple was parted and from that time, there is no discrimination between females and males. We are one in Jesus Christ.

There is neither Jew nor Greek, there is neither slave nor free, there is neither male nor female; for you are all one in Christ Jesus.

-Galatians 3:28 | NKJV

When the Spirit of God fellowships with your soul, He will definitely remind you of Galatians 3:28 and Colossians 3:11. He will never create divisions in the body of Jesus Christ. He will not scatter what Christ has gathered.

Before Genesis 1:1, the Holy Spirit knew divisions would not end the church well because a kingdom that is divided against itself cannot stand. He also knew that the church is the one that would unite all shades of people.

6. Before Genesis 1:1, the fellowship of the Spirit of God was established to assist saints as they share in the sufferings of Jesus Christ.

That I may know Him and the power of His resurrection, and the FELLOWSHIP OF HIS SUFFERINGS, being conformed to His death,

-Philippians 3:10 | NKJV

One of the main pillars of Christianity is suffering. Blessed are you when you are persecuted for righteousness' sake. When you have the fellowship of the Spirit of God, He will lead you into the baptism of fire.

Immediately the Spirit of God came upon God the Son propelling Him to start His ministry, He led Jesus Christ into the wilderness to be tempted by the devil after His 40 days. The fellowship of the Spirit and the Son yielded suffering as a sign of baptism of fire.

Then Jesus was led up by the Spirit into the wilderness to be tempted by the devil.

-Matthew 4:1 | NKJV

If indeed you have the fellowship of the Holy Spirit in you, He will surely lead you into various trials of your faith. The testing of your faith is not there to break or unmake you, but it is there to produce your patience in the faith.

²My brethren, count it all joy when you fall into various trials, ³knowing that the testing of your faith produces patience.

-James 1:2-3 | NKJV

Before Genesis 1:1, the Holy Spirit knew that every saint needed to follow in the steps of God the Son to fulfil all righteousness and one of these steps was the baptism of fire which is all about afflictions.

It was because of the reason of suffering that the Spirit of God became the Comforter so He would comfort those who would mourn because of afflictions and deliver them when the need be. Without mourning or suffering, there is no comfort.

And I will pray the Father, and he shall give you another Comforter, that he may abide with you for ever;

-John 14:16 | KJV

THE WALK OF SANCTIFICATION WITH GOD THE FATHER BEFORE GENESIS 1:1

Therefore, having these promises, beloved, LET US CLEANSE OURSELVES FROM ALL FILTHINESS OF THE FLESH and SPIRIT, perfecting holiness in the fear of God.

-2 Corinthians 7:1 | NKJV

Before the world began, God thought He had to walk with his people in sanctification. There are three main walks with God: sanctification, righteousness, and holiness. They may look the same, but to God, they are not.

Sanctification is mainly about the body. God cares about what we do with our bodies and our surroundings, and we will give account concerning things we did with our bodies.

For we must all appear before the judgment seat of Christ; that every one may receive the THINGS DONE IN HIS BODY, according to that he hath done, whether it be good or bad.

-2 Corinthians 5:10 | NKJV

When God created the universe, the universe was full of junk. The junk of darkness, the junk of formlessness, and the junk of voidness.

God rectified the filthy surrounding of the universe by making sure He made things clean for man to have a nice place to stay. As God cares about our souls, He also cares about the purity of our bodies or what is called sanctification.

Sanctification can be in two folds: the cleanliness of the body and the cleanliness of the soul. But the first move of the Godhead Father was more physical than spiritual. As they say, cleanliness is next to Godliness is so true.

Physical Sanctification

Therefore, having these promises, beloved, LET US CLEANSE OURSELVES FROM ALL FILTHINESS OF THE FLESH and spirit, perfecting holiness in the fear of God.

-2 Corinthians 7:1 | NKJV

As we care about our souls, we must also care for our bodies too. As we care about the neat surroundings of our homes, we must also care about the neat surroundings of our societies, schools, workplaces, churches, and what have you.

If you walk with God, He will never tell you to litter the surroundings even when no one is watching you. At first, I used to litter the surrounding but when I got to know that God wants us to be neat on the inside as He also wants us to be neat outwardly, I repented.

When God wanted to walk in the midst of His people, inasmuch as He wanted them to be sanctified on the inside, He also cared about their physical sanctification. He told them to dig holes, defecate inside, and cover them as a sign of physical sanctification.

[12]"Also you shall have a place outside the camp, where you may go out; [13]and you shall have an implement among your equipment, and when you sit down outside, you shall dig with it and turn and

cover your refuse. ¹⁴For the Lord your God walks in the midst of your camp, to deliver you and give your enemies over to you; therefore your camp shall be holy, that He may see no unclean thing among you, and turn away from you.

-Deuteronomy 23:12-14 | NKJV

Many believers are filthy physically, thinking it is nothing. *You can't walk with God if you are a dirty person.* Many believers don't brush their teeth twice a day and even if they do, they don't do it well.

Many believers who are singles, do not bath twice a day but they want husbands. How can your marriage work if there are many competitors out there who are immaculate? How are you going to maintain your husband if you marry him with your filthiness?

There are many broken marriages of believers not because of adultery but because of filthiness. How can you wash your vagina well as a woman, if you have elongated your natural fingernails with artificial ones?

As much as we think about the cleanliness of our souls, we must also do well to be physically neat. Cleanliness is the state that God the Father wants to meet His people in. It is the first state He wants us to be prepared for, before the spiritual sanctification that comes through the blood of God the Son can begin.

Spiritual Sanctification

Therefore, having these promises, beloved, LET US CLEANSE OURSELVES FROM ALL FILTHINESS OF THE flesh and SPIRIT, perfecting holiness in the fear of God.

-2 Corinthians 7:1 | NKJV

Spiritual sanctification is when the blood of Jesus Christ cleanses the soul of a mortal. We use washing powders to wash our clothes and use detergents to clean our surroundings, but it takes the blood of Jesus Christ as a spiritual cleanser to do the cleaning of the soul.

The blood of animals sacrificed by the Israelites was not enough to cleanse their souls, but could only cover their sins once a year.

¹For the law, having a shadow of the good things to come, and not the very image of the things, can never with these same sacrifices, WHICH THEY OFFER CONTINUALLY YEAR BY YEAR, make those who approach perfect. ²For then would they not have ceased to be offered? FOR THE WORSHIPERS, ONCE PURIFIED, WOULD HAVE HAD NO MORE CONSCIOUSNESS OF SINS. ³But in those sacrifices there is a reminder of sins every year. ⁴FOR IT IS NOT POSSIBLE THAT THE BLOOD OF BULLS AND GOATS COULD TAKE AWAY SINS.

-Hebrews 10:1-4 | NKJV

But the blood of Jesus Christ can wash every stain of sin and can maintain the soul's purity for all eternity.

¹⁰By that will we have been SANCTIFIED THROUGH THE OFFERING OF THE BODY OF JESUS CHRIST ONCE FOR ALL. ¹⁴For by one offering He has PERFECTED FOREVER THOSE WHO ARE BEING SANCTIFIED.

-Hebrews 10:10, 14 | NKJV

If we confess our sins, He is faithful and just to forgive us our sins and to CLEANSE US FROM ALL UNRIGHTEOUSNESS.

-1 John 1:9 | NKJV

5 Things About The Walk Of Sanctification With God The Father Before Genesis 1:1

1. Before Genesis 1:1, God the Father wanted His people to meet Him in the state of sanctification.

[10]Then the Lord said to Moses, "Go to the people and consecrate them today and tomorrow, and let them wash their clothes. [11]And let them be ready for the third day. For on the third day the Lord will come down upon Mount Sinai in the sight of all the people. [12]You shall set bounds for the people all around, saying, 'Take heed to yourselves that you do not go up to the mountain or touch its base. Whoever touches the mountain shall surely be put to death. [13]Not a hand shall touch him, but he shall surely be stoned or shot with an arrow; whether man or beast, he shall not live.' When the trumpet sounds long, they shall come near the mountain."

-Exodus 19:10-13 | NKJV

When God the Father wanted to meet the Israelites, He told Moses to tell the people to sanctify or consecrate themselves physically. If the cleanliness of our bodies does not matter, then why didn't He meet them in their state of uncleanliness?

The focus of the walk with God the Father and His people was more physical than spiritual as planned before the beginning. As believers, we have to free ourselves from all possible forms of dirtiness.

2. Before Genesis 1:1, God the Father wanted His people to sanctify the firstling males of animals.

"ALL THE FIRSTBORN MALES THAT COME FROM YOUR HERD AND YOUR FLOCK YOU SHALL SANCTIFY TO THE LORD YOUR GOD; you shall do no work with the firstborn of your herd, nor shear the firstborn of your flock.

-Deuteronomy 15:19 | NKJV

Before the dispensation of God the Son, animals were used for sacrifices. Even though God was not fully pleased with it, that was the terms He went into with His people, even though He was preparing His Son for the final atonement.

The first fruit of animals mattered to God the Father, and He told His people to sanctify them for Him. God accepting the sacrifice of Abel than Cain was because he sacrificed to God the firstling of the animals he was rearing.

As much as God respects firstborns of people, He also gives respect to first things. God respects you when you prioritise Him concerning the material things you have. Typical example is tithing.

You must set aside your tithe first, before using the rest of the money for your expenses. Don't spend the money and remember that you have not given your tithe before you do so.

You become sanctified when you prioritise God first concerning the things you do because that is His will concerning your life.

3. Before Genesis 1:1, God the Father wanted His people to sanctify unto Him their firstborns.

**"CONSECRATE TO ME ALL THE FIRSTBORN,
whatever opens the womb among the children of
Israel, both of man and beast; it is Mine."**

-Exodus 13:2 | NKJV

Before Genesis 1:1, God knew He would sacrifice His firstborn Son some day, so He did well by preparing Him beforehand. He had much respect for Him because He had a character of gentleness and humility to obey His Word (John 8:55).

Because sanctification was of much importance to God the Father, He told His people to sanctify their firstborns before they could be His property because things that belong to God are all in their state of sanctity.

Before you present people to God, you have to make sure they are in their state of sanctification. There are so many sinners out there not because that is the state they want to be in, but because of the sinful parents who didn't train them well in the Lord.

The firstborns who are sanctified before the Lord spiritually by the blood of God the Son are different from those who are not, even though they all opened the wombs of their mothers.

Even for those who are not sanctified by the training their parents should have given them, are different from the rest of the other children. *A true firstborn is gentle and humble.*

There are so many babies who are thought to have been firstborns but they are not. If you have aborted a baby before and have had any miscarriage also, the baby who comes after that, is not your firstborn.

4. Before Genesis 1:1, God the Father wanted His Priests to be sanctified before beginning ministry.

"Before I formed you in the womb I knew you; before you were born I sanctified you; I ordained you a prophet to the nations."

-Jeremiah 1:5 | NKJV

There are two people in ministry: Ministry by the will of God and ministry by the will of man. For those who are chosen by God (ministry by the will of God), He sanctify them before ordaining them to start ministry, but that is not the case of those who desire it (ministry by the will of man).

This is a faithful saying: If a man desires the position of a bishop, he desires a good work.

-1 Timothy 3:1 | NKJV

Because those who want or desire to be Ministers do not seek for sanctification and ordination from God, they rarely carry out the work to the end. They fall easily, backslide, and even become false Ministers in the end.

It is very important that if God does not choose you to do ministry; you should seek for God to sanctify you and ordain you before you start ministry, because you can't do ministry in sin.

Before Genesis 1:1, God knew those He would choose to carry out His work in all generations and He made sure He equipped them with the sanctification and ordination they needed.

5. Before Genesis 1:1, God the Father wanted His place of worship to be sanctified before He would dwell.

SO I WILL CONSECRATE THE TABERNACLE OF MEETING and the altar. I will also consecrate both Aaron and his sons to minister to Me as priests.
-Exodus 29:44 | NKJV

At first the tabernacle was the physical building for the Father of the Godhead, but now, it is not so. The tabernacle is our bodies, and it is now the dwelling place for the Godhead.

As the Father wanted the physical temple to be sanctified before He dwelt in, He also expects our souls to be sanctified though repentance from all sins so He can dwell in us.

Chapter 20

THE WALK OF RIGHTEOUSNESS WITH GOD THE SON BEFORE GENESIS 1:1

But Jesus answered and said to him, "Permit it to be so now, for thus it is fitting for us to FULFILL ALL RIGHTEOUSNESS." Then he allowed Him.

-Matthew 3:15 | NKJV

Righteousness is the outward purity that comes by careful study of the life of God the Son or the Word of God. Righteousness is the light of a believer that so shines before people. Righteousness is also the good works that people can see a believer doing.

Let your light so shine before men, that they may see your good works and glorify your Father in heaven.

-Matthew 5:16 | NKJV

The righteousness of the people who came before Jesus Christ was not up to its fullness. We heard of people like Job whom the Lord said they were righteous, but if their righteousness were measured, it was not even up to 30%.

They were righteous because their righteousness was more than the generation, they found themselves in. Their dispensation was like a school of dull students whose pass mark is below 30%.

If a student gets 20% more than all the students in the classroom, he is seen as the most brilliant student. But if this same student quits the school and goes to another school of brilliant students who has their pass mark set at 100%, he will be the lowest of them all.

The reason all those who came before God the Son were all sinners and not up to the fullness of Him was that the blood of God the Son had not sanctified them. It is only the blood of Jesus Christ that can usher you into the imputed righteousness of Christianity, which is 30%.

But others fell on good ground and yielded a crop: some a HUNDREDFOLD, some sixty, some thirty.

-Matthew 13:8 | NKJV

God The Son – The Godhead Of Righteousness

Take My yoke upon you and learn from Me, for I am GENTLE and LOWLY IN HEART, and you will find rest for your souls.

-Matthew 11:29 | NKJV

The Godhead who showed us the way of righteousness is God the Son. Righteousness can be seen as light because the light of the world is God the Son. At times righteousness can be seen as salt, which cannot let sin cause us to rot.

[13]"You are the salt of the earth; but if the salt loses its flavor, how shall it be seasoned? It is then good for nothing but to be thrown out and trampled underfoot by men. [14]"You are the light of the world. A city that is set on a hill cannot be hidden.

-Matthew 5:13-14 | NKJV

But the two main evidences of true righteousness are gentleness and humility.

Take My yoke upon you and learn from Me, for I am GENTLE and LOWLY IN HEART, and you will find rest for your souls.

-Matthew 11:29 | NKJV

Because humility is an evidence of righteousness, it made the Godhead of righteousness take the form of a bondservant – humble entity so He could stay among us.

Without humility, you cannot obey the commandments of God. Every sinner is a disobedient person and at that same time, an arrogant person. Without humility and gentleness, which yield obedience to the Word of God, you can never be a righteous person.

Satan is a proud person that is why he cannot obey the commandments of God. If God the Father would have sent Satan to die and save us, he wouldn't have come because of arrogance. It was because of his pride that was why he fell from heaven.

[13].....I will ascend into heaven, I will exalt my throne above the stars of God; I will also sit on the mount of the congregation on the farthest sides of the north; [14]I will ascend above the heights of the clouds, I will be like the Most High.'

-Isaiah 14:13-14 | NKJV

1. Before Genesis 1:1, God the Son knew the Father of faith to whom His seed would carry the descendants of righteousness both physically and spiritually.

[6]And he believed in the Lord, and He accounted it to him for righteousness. blessing I will bless you, and multiplying I will multiply your descendants as the stars of the heaven and as the sand which is on the seashore; and your descendants shall possess the gate of their enemies. In your seed all the nations of the earth shall be blessed, because you have obeyed My voice."

-Genesis 15:6; 22:17-18 | NKJV

The reason Abraham is linked to the dispensation of God the Son in terms of righteousness was that, first of all he was the one who was linked to the birth to Jesus Christ, the Son of the Godhead.

The book of the genealogy of Jesus Christ, the Son of David, the SON OF ABRAHAM:

-Matthew 1:1 | NKJV

Second, Abraham is also the Father of faith who, through his faith in God, was reckoned to him for righteousness. Third, he was the one whose seed was blessed to be a generation of righteousness through faith.

Fourth, it was through the descendants of Abraham that God the Son - the Godhead of righteousness was born. But what was so incredible was that, before Abraham was born, God the Son was already there.

Jesus said to them, "Most assuredly, I say to you, before Abraham was, I AM."

-John 5:58 | NKJV

God the Son knew Abraham before the world began and He chose him to be the one to carry out the seed of the children of righteousness.

2. Before Genesis 1:1, God the Son knew the children of righteousness He would save while He was alive on earth.

Who hath SAVED US, and called us with an holy calling, not according to our works, but according to his own purpose and grace, which was GIVEN US IN CHRIST JESUS BEFORE THE WORLD BEGAN,

-2 Timothy 1:9 | NKJV

God the Son saying He knows His sheep and His sheep also knows Him, tells us that He is Omniscient. Because He knew the living sheep that He had to save on earth, He descended on earth to die and save them with His blood.

He knew that the ministry of reconciliation that He had to carry out was in two folds: for the *living* and the *dead.* He knew His children who would be saved for righteousness while they are alive and not when they are dead.

3. Before Genesis 1:1, God the Son knew the children of righteousness He would save while He was dead.

By whom also He went and preached to the spirits in prison,

-1 Peter 3:18 | NKJV

After the death of Jesus Christ, He went to Hades to preach and save souls because He knew that He had children of righteousness there too. Those who were His children believed, confessed their sins and accepted Him into their lives.

Those who were alive physically saw God the Son in His state of flesh but those who were dead, saw the Spirit of Jesus Christ. Those who were saints in Hades who in the bosom of Abraham at one part of the gulf of fixed, were also saved.

God the Son knew those who could be saved when they are dead and those who could be saved unless they are dead. But in our time now, Jesus Christ doesn't save the dead anymore, but after your death, you will be judged (Hebrews 9:27). There is no salvation in Hades anymore.

4. Before Genesis 1:1, God the Son knew the fate of the disciples He would walk with.

But there are some of you who do not believe." FOR JESUS KNEW FROM THE BEGINNING WHO THEY WERE WHO DID NOT BELIEVE, AND WHO WOULD BETRAY HIM.

-John 6:63 | NKJV

You can't follow the God the Son without Him knowing your state of righteousness from the beginning to the end. Many people became His disciples because of food. Some became His disciples because of healing. Some too became His disciples because He raised the dead.

If you get to know some reasons people follow God the Son now, you will be shocked. Some receive Him into their lives not because of salvation but because they want the woman or man they are chasing, to know that they have changed, but deep inside them they are not.

Some follow God the Son for prosperity, good job, comfort, or children they can give birth. Without the intention of love you have for God the Son, you can never become righteous because the principal mission of God the Son concerns the salvation of the soul and not any other thing.

5. Before Genesis 1:1, God the Son had already written the names of the children of righteousness in His Book of life.

All who dwell on the earth will worship him, whose names have not been written in the Book of Life of the Lamb slain from the foundation of the world.

-Revelation 13:7 | NKJV

Before Genesis 1:1, God the Son already knew those He would use His blood to redeem them. Dying for the world doesn't mean He was dying for animals because animals are also part of the world. The world in John 3:16 represents those souls who were His children but are lost.

Any good shepherd knows His sheep and can identify them even from a distance. God the Son had already written all the names of His children He would save some time to come, even before the world began.

I am the good shepherd; and I know My sheep, and am known by My own.

-John 10:14 | NKJV

6. Before Genesis 1:1, God the Son knew the time He would come to fulfil all righteousness.

BUT WHEN THE FULLNESS OF THE TIME HAD COME, God sent forth His Son, born of a woman, born under the law,

-Galatians 4:4 | NKJV

⁶Then Jesus said to them, "MY TIME HAS NOT YET COME, but your time is always ready. ²⁸After this, JESUS KNOWING THAT ALL THINGS WERE NOW ACCOMPLISHED, that the scripture might be fulfilled, saith, I thirst.

-John 7:6; 19:28 | NKJV

God the Son working with time concerning His ministry, teaches us that, He also knew the time that would be convenient for Him to come as prophesied.

The Godhead work with time. God the Son was active during the time of creation where He was involved using six days in the sight of man and six thousand years in the sight of the Godhead to create.

The prophecy about the coming of the Messiah was time bound. Though it tarried, God the Son was aware of the time He would come to fulfil all righteousness without which no one would be saved.

Before the coming of the Messiah, there was no mortal who had ever lived in this world without committing sin before. He has become the perfect role model for all believers to look up to Him, so they can live also in righteousness.

7. Before Genesis 1:1, God the Son knew the temporal place He would prepare for His children of righteousness.

And Jesus said to him, "Assuredly, I say to you, today you will be with Me in Paradise."

-Luke 23:43 | NKJV

Jesus Christ, telling the malefactor that he would be with Him in Paradise, teaches us that He was the one who created Paradise. It is through God the Son that all things both visible and the invisible were created and can be created.

Which has come to you, as it has also in all the world, and is bringing forth fruit, as it is also among you since the day you heard and knew the grace of God in truth;

-Colossians 1:6 | NKJV

Before the first coming of God the Son, all saints were in a place called Abraham's bosom in the underworld (because he was the Father of faith) after they died. They were not in Paradise because Jesus Christ had not yet died and saved them from the underworld.

8. Before Genesis 1:1, God the Son knew the permanent place He would prepare for His children of righteousness.

[2]In My Father's house are many mansions; if it were not so, I would have told you. I go to prepare a place for you.

³And if I go and prepare a place for you, I will come again and receive you to Myself; that where I am, there you may be also.

-John 14:2-3 | NKJV

New Jerusalem is the permanent place the Godhead decided to prepare for saints or children of righteousness, holiness, and sanctification so they could spend eternity there.

The Son of God knowing His sheep and His sheep knowing Him means that, He knew the total number of people He would prepare places for them to spend their eternity in the New Jerusalem.

Any child of righteousness knows that the earth is just a transient into eternity and he lives his life as a stranger and not as a citizen of the world. He knows his eternal home is New Jerusalem.

9. Before Genesis 1:1, Jesus Christ knew the children of righteousness who would be chosen for the seats of the five-fold ministry.

And He Himself gave some to be apostles, some prophets, some evangelists, and some pastors and teachers,

-Ephesians 4:11 | NKJV

The five-fold ministry is not just offices, as many people know. They are seats that one is enthroned or chosen by God the Son to sit on. You can't enthrone yourself on these seats without being chosen by God the Son. This is because you will lack the protection, anointing, glory, and the grace that the seat has for those who are chosen.

There are many people who could not finish their ministries in the spirit because they chose themselves to be Ministers and not what God the Son intended for them. Even though Jesus Christ can accept you to be a Minister but He will not allow you to sit on the seat He has not prepared for you.

Joshua was the associate of Moses, but because God the Son chose Moses to sit on the seat of Teachers, he received the glory, grace, anointing, and the protection to receive the laws and to teach the Israelites thereof.

Before Genesis 1:1, God the Son already knew and had set the Ministers He would choose to carry out the Apostolic, Prophetic, Evangelistic, Pastoral, and Teaching Ministers and their hierarchal order of importance.

And God has appointed these in the church: FIRST apostles, SECOND prophets, THIRD teachers, AFTER THAT miracles, THEN gifts of healings, helps, administrations, varieties of tongues.

-1 Corinthians 12:28 | NKJV

Chapter 21

THE WALK OF HOLINESS WITH THE SPIRIT OF GOD BEFORE GENESIS 1:1

And declared to be the Son of God with power according to the SPIRIT OF HOLINESS, by the resurrection from the dead.

-Romans 1:4 | NKJV

Holiness is the inner purity of the soul which comes by the cleansing of the blood of God the Son. In the Old Testament, if there was any holiness, it came by the blood of animals, but that was only for a year and it had to be renewed by another sacrifice for another year.

It is only the blood of Jesus Christ that has the power to cleanse the soul forever. True holiness comes by the blood of God the Son and not the blood of animals. This is the essence of the death of God the Son for our souls is to make us holy once and for all.

After the blood of God the Son has finished cleansing the soul, it is now time for the Spirit of holiness to inhabit the temple of the sanctified.

He now fellowships with the soul so He can influence Him with His character of holiness. *The life of a spirit is what the soul adopts, and it is the character of the adopted soul that the body also lives.*

The Coming Upons

At first, the Spirit of holiness or the Spirit of God used to come upon the righteous people but not in them because the blood without sin which should have cleansed the soul was not shed on Calvary yet.

Prophecy As A Manifestation Of Coming Upons

So he went there to Naioth in Ramah. THEN THE SPIRIT OF GOD WAS UPON HIM ALSO, AND HE WENT ON AND PROPHESIED until he came to Naioth in Ramah.

-1 Samuel 19:23 | NKJV

One of the manifestations of the Spirit of holiness coming upon the righteous ones, was prophecy. The moment the Spirit of God came upon someone in the Old Testament, his words changed.

The manifestation of the Holy Spirit has not changed. As He was in the Old Testament, so He is in the New Testament because the Godhead never changes. The person's choice of words is seasoned with salt, and his entire life changes for the better.

The Coming Ins

The Spirit of truth, whom the world cannot receive, because it neither sees Him nor knows Him; but you know Him, for He dwells with you and WILL BE IN YOU.

-John 14:17 | NKJV

After the Spirit of Holiness has seen that the blood of God the Son has cleansed the soul, then, the next move is for Him to dwell in the blood.

BUT YOU ARE NOT IN THE FLESH BUT IN THE SPIRIT, IF INDEED THE SPIRIT OF GOD DWELLS IN YOU.....

-Romans 8:9 | NKJV

The reason the world cannot receive the Spirit of holiness is that the blood of God the Son has not yet cleansed their souls.

As God the Son came for lost souls or unbelievers, the mission of the Spirit of holiness is for believers. It is in those temples that He can dwell in and lead them into holiness, making them what we call, 'CHRISTIAN.'

Heart – The Master Bedroom Of The Spirit Of Holiness

Who also has sealed us and given us the SPIRIT IN OUR HEARTS as a guarantee.

-2 Corinthians 1:22 | NKJV

The Godhead specifically created us so He would stay in us someday. But there is a special place in us that spirits love to dwell in so they can ensure longevity of inhabitancy. We have spirits that best thrive in fresh water, brackish water, the sea, rocks, mountains, sky, trees, animals, etc.

The Spirit of God also has the best place He can thrive in the temple of saints. The heart is the master bedroom for the Spirit of God, where He can thrive in best and lead His people into all acts of holiness.

The True Worship

.....The true worshipers will worship the Father in spirit and truth; for the Father is seeking such to worship Him. God is Spirit, and those who worship Him must worship in spirit and truth."

-John 4:23-24 | NKJV

The true worship is when the Kingdom of God (Holy Spirit) rules in the affairs of the Kingdom of heaven (Christianity or the church).

The true worship is also in two folds: Spirit and Truth. The righteousness of the Holy Spirit is solely based on Truth. He is not a Godhead who can lie. It is impossible. As it is impossible for Him to lie, it is also impossible for Him to sin.

Those who have the Holy Spirit in them are the ones who worship God truly and not falsely. There are many false worshippers out there who think they are worshipping God, but they are not.

.....NOW IF ANYONE DOES NOT HAVE THE SPIRIT OF CHRIST, HE IS NOT HIS.

-Romans 8:9 | NKJV

The Prophesy Of The True Worship

"And it shall come to pass afterward that I will pour out My Spirit on all flesh; your sons and your daughters shall prophesy, your old men shall dream dreams, your young men shall see visions.

-Joel 2:28 | NKJV

The true worship has since been prophesied about. One thing we need to note is that God cannot be worshipped with flesh and blood because worship in carnality cannot please God.

From the Old Testament, the vision of the true worship was prophesied, and through those times, the Godhead was preparing for such a time to come so it can be pleasing to the Godhead.

The Promise To The Woman Of Samaria

But the hour is coming…..

-John 4:23 | NKJV

When God the Son met the woman at the well, because He was part of the Godhead, He re-echoed the prophecy about the coming of the true worship that had long been expected.

He prophesied to her about the soon coming of the Spirit of the Godhead who would bring about the true worship the Godhead was seeking in the lives of their children.

The Promise To The Crowd

[37]On the last day, that great day of the feast, Jesus stood and cried out, saying, "If anyone thirsts, let him come to Me and drink. [38]He who believes in Me, as the Scripture has said, out of his heart will flow rivers of living water." [39]But this He spoke concerning the Spirit, whom those believing in Him would receive; for the Holy Spirit was not yet given, because Jesus was not yet glorified.

-John 7:37-39 | NKJV

After telling the woman of Samaria the promise of the coming of the Holy Spirit who would make His children worship the Godhead in truth and in Spirit, God the Son went on to re-echo the same promise to the crowd too.

The Promise To The Disciples

⁴**And being assembled together with them, He commanded them not to depart from Jerusalem, but to wait for the Promise of the Father, "which," He said, "you have heard from Me; ⁵for John truly baptized with water, but you shall be baptized with the Holy Spirit not many days from now." ⁶Therefore, when they had come together, they asked Him, saying, "Lord, will You at this time restore the kingdom to Israel?" ⁷And He said to them, "It is not for you to know times or seasons which the Father has put in His own authority. ⁸But you shall receive power when the Holy Spirit has come upon you; and you shall be witnesses to Me in Jerusalem, and in all Judea and Samaria, and to the end of the earth."**

-Acts 1:4-8 | NKJV

Before the ascension of God the Son, He did the last re-echoing of the promise to the coming of the Holy Spirit - the Godhead behind the true worship.

The Fulfilment Of The Promise

¹**When the Day of Pentecost had fully come, they were all with one accord in one place. ²And suddenly there came a sound from heaven, as of a rushing mighty wind, and it filled the whole house where they were sitting. ³Then there appeared to them divided tongues, as of fire, and one sat upon each of them. ⁴And they were all filled with the Holy Spirit and began to speak with other tongues, as the Spirit gave them utterance.**

-Acts 2:1-4 | NKJV

After Jesus Christ told the disciples to assemble themselves in Jerusalem in wait for the coming of the Spirit of God, the promise was finally fulfilled on the day of Pentecost (a Jewish holiday observed on the sixth of Sivan and by Orthodox and Conservative Jews in the Diaspora; also on the seventh of Sivan in commemoration of the revelation of the Ten Commandments at Mount Sinai).

1. Before Genesis 1:1, the Spirit of holiness of the Godhead knew how He would empower the Word of God to convert lost souls into children of holiness.

> **⁴And MY SPEECH AND MY PREACHING were not with persuasive words of human wisdom, BUT IN DEMONSTRATION OF THE SPIRIT AND OF POWER, ⁵that your FAITH SHOULD NOT BE IN THE WISDOM OF MEN BUT IN THE POWER OF GOD.**
>
> **-1 Corinthians 2:4-5 | NKJV**

As mortals, we cannot change anyone. They can appear to us as changed people, but in them, they are not. No wonder many believers do not sin in the church building where the Pastor and the congregation are, but they sin when they are in places when these people are not around.

The Spirit of God is the One who changes people, but He cannot do so without the Word of God. The Spirit of God works hand-in-hand with the Gospel, convicting and converting lost souls into children of holiness.

There are two things about the Spirit of God: His *presence* and His *power. You can have the power without the presence, but you can't have the presence without the power.* The presence is the Person of the Holy Spirit, but the power is His operation or anointing.

Signs that follow the Gospel, is the demonstration of the power of the Holy Spirit. If you truly possess the Holy Spirit in you, there must be signs that must follow you.

¹⁷And these signs will follow those who believe: In My name they will cast out demons; they will speak with new tongues; ¹⁸they will take up serpents; and if they drink anything deadly, it will by no means hurt them; they will lay hands on the sick, and they will recover."

-Mark 16:17-18 | NKJV

Sometimes we are mistaken when we see the signs of the power of the Holy Spirit in operation even though the life of the person is not right in our eyes in terms of moral conduct.

Before the fallen angels were overthrown from heaven, God did not take the power He gave them, but He allowed them to operate with it after their overthrow, even though they rebelled against Him.

The power can be given as a gift and you can be used by the Spirit of God to preach the Gospel and save souls, but if the vessel doesn't repent from the sins he commits, he will perish.

²¹"Not everyone who says to Me, Lord, Lord,' shall enter the kingdom of heaven, but he who does the will of My Father in heaven. ²²MANY WILL SAY TO ME IN THAT DAY, 'LORD, LORD, HAVE WE NOT PROPHESIED IN YOUR NAME, CAST OUT DEMONS IN YOUR NAME, AND DONE MANY WONDERS IN YOUR NAME?'

[23]And then I will declare to them, 'I NEVER KNEW YOU; DEPART FROM ME, YOU WHO PRACTICE LAWLESSNESS!'

-Matthew 7:21-23 | NKJV

2. Before Genesis 1:1, the Spirit of holiness of the Godhead knew the fruits He would bear in the lives of His children.

[22]But the fruit of the Spirit is love, joy, peace, longsuffering, kindness, goodness, faithfulness, [23]gentleness, self-control. Against such there is no law.

-Galatians 5:22-23 | NKJV

The manifestation of the presence of the Holy Spirit in you is not new speaking of tongues, as many people know. How can you have the Holy Spirit and yet bear fruits of the flesh such as sexual immorality, idolatry, heresies, and many more?

[19]Now the works of the flesh are evident, which are: adultery, fornication, uncleanness, lewdness, [20]idolatry, sorcery, hatred, contentions, jealousies, outbursts of wrath, selfish ambitions, dissensions, heresies, [21]envy, murders, drunkenness, revelries, and the like; of which I tell you beforehand, just as I also told you in time past, that those who practice such things will not inherit the kingdom of God.

-Galatians 5:19-21 | NKJV

The manifestation of the presence of the Holy Spirit is the nine fruits He bears. If you have the Holy Spirit, we must see you bearing the fruits of love, joy, peace, long-suffering, kindness, goodness, faithfulness, gentleness, and self-control.

Even so, every good tree bears good fruit, but a bad tree bears bad fruit.

-Matthew 7:17 | NKJV

One caution we need to take note is that, during judgement, we will be verified if we have all the nine fruits in us. If we bear eight fruits, leaving just one fruit, we will not have eternal life. It is a must you bear all the nine fruits so we can have eternal life.

Before Genesis 1:1, the Spirit of God knew the nine fruits He would bear in the lives of His children. The totality of all the nine fruits in a person is what gives the evidence that the person's soul is holy.

3. Before Genesis 1:1, the Spirit of holiness of the Godhead knew the gifts He would give to His children.

[8]For to one is given the word of wisdom through the Spirit, to another the word of knowledge through the same Spirit, [9]to another faith by the same Spirit, to another gifts of healings by the same Spirit, [10]to another the working of miracles, to another prophecy, to another discerning of spirits, to another different kinds of tongues, to another the interpretation of tongues. [11]But one and the same Spirit works all these things, distributing to each one individually as He wills.

-1 Corinthians 12:8-11 | NKJV

The difference between the gifts and the fruits of the Holy Spirit is that the fruits are the evidence of the presence of the Holy Spirit in a person, but the gift is just the manifestation of the power of the Holy Spirit.

Like a tree, the gifts of the Holy Spirit are the leaves He bears, and the fruits are the nine virtues He bears.

You can have the gift(s) of the Spirit of God when He is living with you and not in you. If we cast our minds back to the Old Testament, the Spirit of God was not dwelling in them but He was dwelling upon them.

Dwelling upon them, He still gave them gifts to operate with. Some were given the gift of prophecy, thus the Prophets and some anointed Kings. Some were given the gift of wisdom as in the case of King Solomon and gifted artisans for the carrying out of godly tasks.

Before Genesis 1:1, the Spirit of the Godhead knew how He would distribute His gifts to His children concerning His own will, for the profit of the church, and to the glory of God.

4. Before Genesis 1:1, the Spirit of holiness of the Godhead knew how He would manifest His lifestyle of holiness.

Whoever has been born of God does not sin, for His seed remains in him; and he cannot sin, because he has been born of God.

-1 John 3:9 | NKJV

The evidence of the presence of the Holy Spirit in someone is holiness. It is impossible for someone who has the Holy Spirit to sin. As an orange tree naturally cannot produce banana fruits, so the soul of someone who is holy, cannot commit sin.

A good tree cannot bear bad fruit, nor can a bad tree bear good fruit.

-Matthew 7:18 | NKJV

Someone can be righteous outwardly for all to see, but you may not be in the person's mind and you can't see what is in the person's heart. Holiness is inwardly, and it takes the fellowship of the Holy Spirit to lead the soul into.

Before Genesis 1:1, the Spirit of God thought how He would restore man to his original state of holiness, which he would lose in the Garden of Eden some time to come.

5. Before Genesis 1:1, the Spirit of holiness of the Godhead knew the language He would give to His people to speak.

And these signs will follow those who believe: In My name they will cast out demons; they will speak with NEW TONGUES;

-Mark 16:17 | NKJV

Christianity is a nation or a kingdom. Every nation has her own language she speaks. The language every citizen of Christianity speaks is new speaking of tongues.

There is difference between *different tongues* and *new tongues*. For different kinds of tongues, it is interpretable, but that is not the case of new tongues. This is not what many people don't understand well.

Different kinds of tongues are given to someone as the Spirit of God wills, which is optional, but the new speaking of tongues is given to all saints as a mandatory language. You can't be in a nation without speaking her language.

Before Genesis 1:1, the Spirit of God knew when He would give all languages out to the nations of the earth. He thought before the beginning to confuse the language of the people of Babel when they would try to build a tower towards heaven.

⁶And the Lord said, "Indeed the people are one and they all have one language, and this is what they begin to do; now nothing that they propose to do will be withheld from them. ⁷COME, LET US GO DOWN AND THERE CONFUSE THEIR LANGUAGE, THAT THEY MAY NOT

UNDERSTAND ONE ANOTHER'S SPEECH." ⁸So the Lord scattered them abroad from there over the face of all the earth, and they ceased building the city. ⁹Therefore its name is called Babel, because there the Lord confused the language of all the earth; and from there the Lord scattered them abroad over the face of all the earth.

-Genesis 11:6-9 | NKJV

Before Genesis 1:1, He thought that, He had to give all languages to the people of the earth, but had to reserve new tongues for the nation that would be founded by God the Son some time to come, which is Christianity.

6. Before Genesis 1:1, the Spirit of holiness of the Godhead knew how He would help His children to work out their own salvation.

¹²Therefore, my beloved, as you have always obeyed, not as in my presence only, but now much more in my absence, work out your own salvation with fear and trembling; ¹³FOR IT IS GOD WHO WORKS IN YOU BOTH TO WILL AND TO DO FOR HIS GOOD PLEASURE.

-Philippians 2:12-13 | NKJV

The Spirit of the Godhead is the helper of the saints' salvation. We wanted to serve God in the Old Testament, but we were not having the Helper in us who would help us worship the Godhead in Spirit and in truth.

We were not true worshippers because the Spirit of God who should be our Helper was not dwelling in us to work through us what pleased the Godhead.

What we need to take note of is that, even though the Spirit of God is our Helper, that does not mean we should be dormant in our works of salvation. Our fleshes must be willing and not weak, so the Spirit of God who is also willing to help us can do so for holiness to be achieved.

Many believers, after having the Holy Spirit no longer pray, read, meditate, or study their Bibles, go to church any longer, evangelise or win souls or make any effort to do so for. They expect the Spirit of God to do all the dirty works while they go on holidays.

This same attitude is what many husbands have in their marriages. At first that they were bachelors, they used to sweep their rooms, do all the cleaning and washing and at times, they cook but when they marry, they leave all the work for the wives to do thinking as their helpers, they need to do everything for them.

The Spirit of God is not here to do everything for us as we sit down idle without putting in any effort. It is not everybody that the Spirit dwells in him or her.

You can pray for Him to come into you, but if you are not part of those who have been elected, knowing that you would end in the flesh and not in the Spirit even before Genesis 1:1, will not dwell in you.

7. Before Genesis 1:1, the Spirit of holiness of the Godhead knew how He would bear witness with our souls that we are true children of God.

> **The Spirit Himself bears witness with our spirit that we are children of God,**
>
> -Romans 8:16 | NKJV

Fear and doubt or unbelief are not in the Spirit of God. He is full of faith and anyone He is dwelling in, is not someone who is fearful, doubtful or double-minded. The sound mind of the Spirit of God is a mind of faith.

For God has not given us a spirit of fear, but of power and of love and of a sound mind.

-2 Timothy 1:7 | NKJV

It is the Spirit of God who is full of faith, witnessing to the one whom He is dwelling in that he or she is a child of God. It is Him who gives power or right to the one He is dwelling in to be a child of God.

But as many as received Him, to them He gave the right to become children of God, to those who believe in His name:

-John 1:12 | NKJV

He bears witness to the person's soul as He fellowships with Him so he can be rest assured of his or her certainty of salvation.

8. Before Genesis 1:1, the Spirit of holiness of the Godhead knew the children of holiness He would seal them for eternal life.

[13]In Him you also trusted, after you heard the word of truth, the gospel of your salvation; in whom also, having believed, YOU WERE SEALED WITH THE HOLY SPIRIT OF PROMISE,
[14]WHO IS THE GUARANTEE OF OUR INHERITANCE until the redemption of the purchased possession, to the praise of His glory.

-Ephesians 1:13-14 | NKJV

As there are children of the devil or darkness, so are there children of light or of the Lord, and they are manifest based on lifestyles they live.

In this the children of God and the children of the devil are manifest: Whoever does not practice righteousness is not of God, nor is he who does not love his brother.

-1 John 3:10 | NKJV

There is always something that identifies a woman and what identifies a man, and that is the gender. Even if you are a hermaphrodite, you will have one gender than is superior to the other.

For children of darkness, what identifies them is their continual lifestyle in sin, and what sets children of darkness is the continual lifestyle of holiness inwardly, and righteousness which is outwardly. Before this can be, it is the spirit that lives in these two people that seals their way of life.

He who is unjust, let him be unjust still; he who is filthy, let him be filthy still; he who is righteous, let him be righteous still; he who is holy, let him be holy still."

-Revelation 22:11 | NKJV

The devil has his mark for his children, and the Lord also has His mark that identifies His children. It is this seal of the Spirit of God that qualifies the children of light as candidates of eternal life and it is the seal of the spirit of the devil that makes children of darkness candidates of eternal damnation or the second death.

Before Genesis 1:1, the Spirit of the Godhead had already sealed the people He would seal them for eternal life. He knew the quantity of people who would have eternal life even before the world began.

9. Before Genesis 1:1, the Spirit of holiness of the Godhead already knew the children He would inhabit.

For you did not receive the spirit of bondage again to fear, but you received the Spirit of adoption by whom we cry out, "Abba, Father."

-Romans 8:15 | NKJV

It is not enough to have the Holy Spirit living upon you, with you or on you. It is very important to have the Spirit of God living in you. It is the Spirit of God that will make you abide in the Word of God and the Word of God abide in you because the Word of God is Jesus Christ.

Now the Lord is the Spirit; and where the Spirit of the Lord is, there is liberty.

-2 Corinthians 3:17 | NKJV

It is one thing to be a believer and another thing to be a Christian. A believer is someone who has the Holy Spirit living upon, with, and on him or her. A Christian is someone who has the Holy Spirit living in him or her.

The reason the Holy Spirit can live with, upon, or on you is that everyone was created by God to fulfil a certain purpose only God wants, whether evil or good. The person can fulfil God's purpose, but the person will not be a child of God.

Because God the Son had already written the names of those who are His children even before the world began and the Spirit of God has also sealed them, it is those who are elected to be children of God that the Spirit of God will stay in them and this was already predetermined before Genesis 1:1.

10. Before Genesis 1:1, the Spirit of holiness of the Godhead knew how He would anoint His children for ministry.

¹⁸**"THE SPIRIT OF THE LORD IS UPON ME, because HE HAS ANOINTED ME to preach the gospel to the poor; He has sent Me to heal the brokenhearted, to proclaim liberty to the captives and recovery of sight to the blind, to set at liberty those who are oppressed; ¹⁹to proclaim the acceptable year of the Lord."**

-Luke 4:18-19 | NKJV

How God ANOINTED JESUS OF NAZARETH WITH THE HOLY SPIRIT AND WITH POWER, who went about doing good and healing all who were oppressed by the devil, for God was with Him.

-Acts 10:38 | NKJV

God the Son, who was fully man and fully God, didn't begin His ministry without the anointing of the Spirit of God. The Spirit of God came upon Him because He was the Apostle of the Old Testament, because He was born under the law.

But when the fullness of the time had come, God sent forth His Son, born of a woman, BORN UNDER THE LAW,

-Galatians 4:4 | NKJV

Many people know the anointing as some oil that is put on someone by another Minister, ordaining the supposed anointed person for ministry. *The anointing is not a thing, but a person.*

If you read Acts 10:38, God the Father didn't anoint God the Son with any object of anointing but the subject of the anointing who is not just a force but a Person.

The anointing we too receive is not just a physical pouring of oil for ordination but the Person of the Spirit of God who does that.

11. Before Genesis 1:1, the Spirit of holiness of the Godhead knew the deep things of the Godhead He would reveal to His children.

But God has revealed them to us through His Spirit. For the Spirit searches all things, yes, the deep things of God.

-1 Corinthians 2:10 | NKJV

The Godhead doesn't want us to be shallow. When Son of man met Peter, He told him to cast his net into the place of the deep so he could catch fish. The seed of the Word of God needs a deeper heart to contain the tap roots of the deeper things of God.

DEEP CALLS UNTO DEEP at the noise of Your waterfalls; all Your waves and billows have gone over me.

-Psalms 42:7 | NKJV

Some fell on stony places, where they did not have much earth; and they immediately sprang up because they had no depth of earth.

-Matthew 13:5 | NKJV

Before Genesis 1:1, the Godhead chose the Spirit of God as the Godhead who would reveal the deep things of God to their children. During creation, we saw the evidence of Him upon the face of the deep revealing to us that He was in charge of the deep things of God.

If we truly want to understand the Word of God, we can't do so without the Spirit of God. He is the One who knows all mysteries of Godliness and the Word of God. You can read the Bible, but without the Holy Spirit, you will never understand it.

12. Before Genesis 1:1, the Spirit of holiness of the Godhead already knew the time He would leave earth with those He had inhabited into their eternal destination.

.....But whether there are prophecies, they will fail; whether there are tongues, they will cease; whether there is knowledge, it will vanish away.

-1 Corinthians 13:8 | NKJV

The earth is not the dwelling place of the Spirit of God. It is because of the blood of God the Son that is why He is dwelling in the temple of His children.

Prophecies, divers' kinds of tongues, and knowledge as gifts of the Holy Spirit vanishing away is a clear sign about the end of His work.

As the reigns of God the Father and God the Son ended on earth, the reign of the Spirit of God will also end finally when the second coming of Jesus Christ is due. It is the Spirit of God in you who will rapture you into the sky with the Lord.

Before Genesis 1:1, the Spirit of the Godhead knew the time His fellowship in the lives of the saints would end temporally on earth. He knew that the eternal destination of the saints was New Jerusalem, even before the world began where they would spend eternal life.